FRAMEWORKS

SKYSCRAPERS

and HIGH RISES

Shana Priwer

Cynthia Phillips

Sharpe Focus
an imprint of M.E. Sharpe, Inc.

Sharpe Focus
An imprint of M.E. Sharpe, Inc.
80 Business Park Drive
Armonk, NY 10504
www.sharpe-focus.com

Library of Congress Cataloging-in-Publication Data

Phillips, Cynthia, 1973–
  Skyscrapers and high rises / Cynthia Phillips and Shana Priwer.
     p. cm. — (Frameworks)
  Includes bibliographical references and index.
  ISBN 978-0-7656-8121-8 (hardcover : alk. paper)
 1. Skyscrapers—Juvenile literature. 2. Tall buildings—Juvenile
literature. 3. Structural design—Juvenile literature. 4. Building
failures—Juvenile literature. I. Priwer, Shana. II. Title.

NA6230.P45 2008
720'.483—dc22

                               2007040701

Editor: Peter Mavrikis
Production Manager: Henrietta Toth
Editorial Assistant and Photo Research: Alison Morretta
Program Coordinator: Cathy Prisco
Design: Patrice Sheridan
Line Art: FoxBytes

Printed in Malaysia

9 8 7 6 5 4 3 2 1

PHOTO CREDITS : Cover: Photographer's Choice/Getty Images; title page: Stone/Getty Images; pages 6, 15, 20, 27, 32, 36, 42, 50, 55, 92, 96, 98: Hulton Archive/Getty Images; pages 8, 28: Courtesy of the Francis Loeb Library, Graduate School of Design, Harvard University; pages 10, 23, 25, 29, 37, 38, 39, 40, 44, 46, 52, 64, 67, 72, 73, 81: FoxBytes; pages 11, 22, 43, 58, 87, 102: Time Life Pictures/Getty Images; pages 12, 29, 53, 54, 57, 94, 95: Library of Congress; pages 14, 31: Altrendo/Getty Images; page 17: New York Public Library; page 18: Roger Viollet/Getty Images; page 26: Dorling Kindersley/Getty Images; pages 33, 99, 100, 103: Associated Press; pages 34, 77: Getty Images; pages 48, 62, 70, 91: Photographer's Choice/Getty Images; page 59: Gallo Images/Getty Images; page 61: Asia Images/Getty Images; pages 65, 68, 71, 78, 82, 97: Stone/Getty Images; page 66: First Light/Getty Images; pages 74, 83: AFP/Getty Images; pages 84, 89: Science Faction/Getty Images; page 86: Taxi/Getty Images; back cover: Photographer's Choice/Getty Images.

CONTENTS

ABOUT FRAMEWORKS

Architecture has undergone sweeping changes since the beginning of time. In biblical times, most architecture was temporary because it accommodated nomadic populations. As communities began to grow roots, so did their architecture. Whether residential, commercial, religious, or civic, structures of permanence slowly appeared on the global landscape.

Over time, specific aesthetics and structural techniques developed in different parts of the world. Advancements in physical sciences allowed engineers to create increasingly complex works that challenged previous notions. Temples became more elaborate, buildings grew ever taller, and bridges spanned bodies of water that only boats had dared to cross before. Once science and design crossed paths, there was no turning back.

The goal of the FRAMEWORKS series is to provide insight into the science behind the structures that are part of our everyday lives. For example, dams use advanced hydroelectric technology to produce power. The Egyptian pyramids paved new paths in the transport and construction of stone structures. Basic concepts in mathematics, physics, and engineering help to illustrate the science that supports the creation of such structures.

This series assumes no prior knowledge of advanced math and physics, but rather builds the reader's understanding by explaining scientific concepts in common terms, as well as basic equations. Engaging examples illustrate ideas such as mass, force, speed, and energy. Case studies from real-world projects demonstrate the concepts.

SKYSCRAPERS AND HIGH RISES details the development of the sky-scraper. The skyscraper comes from very humble roots; short brick buildings were actually the world's first "high rises." As technological and engineering knowledge advanced by leaps and bounds, buildings grew to heights that had previously been impossible to achieve. Perhaps most important was the invention of structural steel, which allowed for the development of the sky-scraper. In the late nineteenth century, English inventor Sir Henry Bessemer developed a process for mass-produced steel, a building material that is well suited to creating tall, thin, strong structures.

Of course, steel alone cannot create a skyscraper. As steel frames quickly came into common use for super-tall buildings, new materials were necessary to apply to the buildings' exteriors. The brick that had been a primary building material for centuries worked well for lower floors, but was too heavy to use seventy stories up. Initially, masonry panels were used to enclose the sides of tall skyscrapers. Later, metal and glass became the primary materials used in their facades.

Another important invention that allowed skyscrapers to be used to their full potential was the elevator. At the 1854 World's Fair in New York City, Elisha Graves Otis demonstrated his safety elevator, complete with a special braking mechanism that made the elevator safe for human transport. The safety elevator quickly became a necessity for any high-rise building. The invention of the telephone also facilitated people's use of tall buildings. For the first time, communication within a tall building was possible without sending messengers running up and down many flights of stairs.

Skyscraper design has evolved considerably since its inception. Due to advances in construction materials and more daring designs, skyscrapers continue to grow ever taller. With these new heights come new structural requirements. Skyscrapers must be designed to resist wind, earthquakes, and other lateral forces in ways that were less relevant for shorter structures.

While the demise of some skyscrapers has been accidental, others have been torn down to make room for larger and more modern buildings. Photographs and memories are all that remain of some of the world's greatest skyscrapers. But those that have been preserved over the years stand as living testaments to building innovation.

The FRAMEWORKS series provides an entertaining and educational approach to the science of building. Read on to learn about the ways in which science literally supports our built environment.

A BRIEF HISTORY OF SKYSCRAPERS

In the history of invention, specific individuals often receive credit for the development of innovations that helped move society forward. Wilbur and Orville Wright, for example, made significant headway in the development of the airplane and are partly responsible for its initial burst of development. Benjamin Franklin relied on past inventions when he developed the bifocal lens, yet its ultimate invention is attributed to Franklin alone. Similarly, Alexander Graham Bell is known as the father of the modern telephone.

The path that led to the creation of the skyscraper was inherently different. No single genius is considered solely responsible for skyscrapers as we know them. The development of super-tall architecture was a collaborative venture that involved architects, engineers, mechanics, builders, masons, welders, and many other individuals.

The identity of the "first" skyscraper is the subject of much debate. Some of the first tall buildings were not skyscrapers in any modern sense of the word. Chicago was the site of some of the earliest attempts to build tall buildings after the Great Chicago Fire of 1871. The seven-story Marshall Field Wholesale Store in Chicago, designed by Henry Hobson Richardson and built in 1885, was constructed of load-bearing masonry. Richardson's building, though not the tallest structure of the time, did

Sky-high construction takes place on the Empire State Building, 1930.

point out limitations of the current technology and was therefore a key component in the development of the skyscraper.

The Home Insurance Company Building in Chicago, also built in 1885, was the first to use the new technology of steel-girder construction. Designed by American master architect William Le Baron Jenney, the building had one of the first load-bearing structural cage frames. It was much lighter than a comparable masonry building would have been. Stone masonry buildings were quite heavy and gave the appearance of a solid, structurally sound building. Steel is a physically lighter material, and because of the use of thinner structural members, the buildings using this new technology seemed less dense than their stone counterparts. Inspectors even worried about its stability and at one point called for a

The Marshall Field Wholesale Store Building, an early high-rise, was a predecessor to the skyscraper.

stop in construction. Other groundbreaking buildings followed, such as Chicago's Tacoma Building, built in 1887–1889, and the New York World Building, built in 1890.

The individuals responsible for these masterpieces had many obstacles to overcome, and their collective solutions made possible the development of buildings that grew ever taller. Making skyscrapers habitable proved to be one of the most challenging problems in the entire design process. As developments in building materials and transportation progressed, taller buildings appeared in large cities across the United States, notably New York and Chicago. Innovations in steel and glass allowed for taller buildings, and the development of the Otis elevator allowed people to reach and occupy the upper levels of these structures. As technology and design rose to new heights, so did the skyscrapers.

Skyscrapers are an outcome of humanity's obsession with magnificent surroundings. An examination of the Wonders of the Ancient World, which include the Great Pyramid of Giza in Egypt and the Greek Colossus of Rhodes, reveals that from the very beginning of documented history, people have been interested in beautiful design. Skyscrapers are a significant part of this legacy and will continue to challenge the talents of engineers and architects into the future.

SKYSCRAPER OR HIGH RISE?

How do skyscrapers and high rises differ? While the terms are often used interchangeably, they are not exactly the same thing. Although the word *skyscraper* originated from mundane roots, modern usage has applied the term to a class of tall buildings. Skyscraper describes any very tall building that can be occupied. The term was first applied to buildings erected in the late nineteenth century. The height requirement for a classification as a skyscraper has changed over time. Today, anything taller than 800 feet (250 meters) is generally considered a skyscraper.

A high rise, on the other hand, is described by the Emporis Data Committee, which maintains building information for cities around the world, as any building taller than 115 feet (35 meters) that is divided into

By comparing skyscraper heights, it is possible to see how far technology has improved the ability to create super-tall structures.

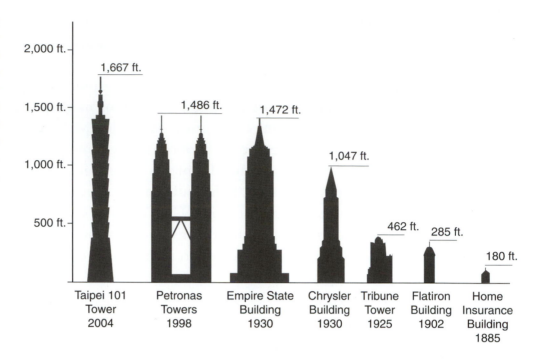

separate floors. By this definition, every skyscraper is a high rise, but the converse is not true. The term skyscraper has connotations of grandeur, as a soaring structure that seems to reach to the very heavens in a way that a mere high rise cannot hope to emulate.

ORIGIN OF THE TERM

Skyscraper was originally a nautical term that referred to a moon sail, a triangular sail used on certain types of sailing ships, such as the elegant nineteenth-century clipper ships. The moon sail was the topmost sail and, as it seemed to scrape the sky, was called a skyscraper. There are also anecdotal references to the word skyscraper being used to describe exceptionally high-flying birds and particularly tall hats in the nineteenth century.

OVERCOMING OBSTACLES

Load-bearing masonry buildings reached new heights in the 1880s and 1890s, but it became clear that there were physical limitations to this type of construction that could not be overcome. If buildings were going to reach higher than a few stories, something stronger than bricks or masonry was needed to support them.

Enter flexible steel framing. The Bethlehem Steel Company, one of the largest suppliers to the U.S. shipbuilding industry, was one of several manufacturers that were developing new, innovative processes for manufacturing steel in the late 1800s.

The introduction of steel, which is stronger and lighter in weight than iron, made it possible for buildings to reach higher than ever before. Around the same time, reinforced concrete and the concept of the curtain wall were developed. A curtain wall is a building's outer covering that is supported by the steel frame structure; its purpose is to protect the building's interior from

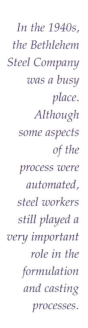

In the 1940s, the Bethlehem Steel Company was a busy place. Although some aspects of the process were automated, steel workers still played a very important role in the formulation and casting processes.

rain, wind, snow, and various other conditions. Unlike its load-bearing predecessors, a curtain wall only had to support its own weight. Heavy masonry siding could only be built to a certain height because the weight of these materials was such that, to build higher, the foundation walls below would have to have been extremely thick. Lighter curtain walls added less load to the structure, and, as a result, could be built higher than their stone counterparts. The first true curtain walls appeared in the early twentieth century. San Francisco architect Willis Polk designed the Hallidie Building, which used a system of exterior glass that was non–load-bearing. This spawned a wave of new development, but also revealed some immediate problems. In an era before air conditioning or insulated glass, Polk's buildings became a sort of sauna for their unfortunate occupants. Luckily, the necessary technology to make curtain walls really work was soon to come.

Materials were not the only obstacles to building taller buildings. Once all those floors were constructed, how were people going to get to them? As buildings grew to more than a few stories tall, staircases became impractical as a primary means of accessing the top floors. The invention of the safety elevator by Elisha Otis in 1854 opened up new possibilities for vertical travel. Building designs began to incorporate space for an elevator shaft, and advances in elevator design soon resulted in safer passenger transportation.

Why were taller buildings necessary? By the 1880s, space was becoming more and more precious in large cities, while at the same time more work and living space was required. Chicago's population growth was unprecedented, increasing from 112,000 in 1860 to nearly 300,000 in 1870.

Without elevators, the upper floors of skyscrapers would have been largely inaccessible.

Then tragedy struck. On October 8, 1871, the Great Chicago Fire left nearly one-third of the city homeless, destroying more than 18,000 buildings. Chicago began rebuilding almost immediately. The city bounced back not by simply replacing what was lost, but by outdoing the old Chicago. Given the opportunity to rebuild huge sections of the city, architects and designers embraced the newly available technology and built structures that reached for the sky. Never a city to be left behind, New York responded in kind, and the trend in these two metropolises was soon followed across the country.

THE LOGISTICS OF CONSTRUCTION

The construction of a skyscraper is a truly massive endeavor. After the land is secured, design established, and code clearances met, the site is excavated. To anchor a skyscraper firmly into the soil, a huge pit must be dug for the foundation, requiring large amounts of soil to be removed and placed elsewhere. Digging a skyscraper foundation is no small effort. As the soil is removed, a retaining wall is typically constructed to keep the remaining earth from moving at the edges of the hole. These retaining walls are impressive structures. A trench is dug and filled with slurry, a type of wet clay. As the trench grows sufficiently deep, steel pieces are lowered into it for reinforcement, and the slurry is piped back out, ready to be used for the next trench. If bedrock is found close to the surface, it must first be removed so that a smooth surface can be created for the foundation.

An important consideration in any skyscraper construction plan is what to do with the dirt left from the excavation of the foundation pit. One solution is to truck the dirt out to another location. Another is for the dirt to end up in its own backyard in landfills. Some parts of New York City, for example, are built on landfill that was created with the dirt excavated in the construction of skyscrapers. The original World Trade Center towers, constructed in the 1970s, produced about one million cubic yards (750,000 cubic meters) of soil. This material, deposited into the Hudson River, resulted in the creation of more than 20 acres of habitable land.

When digging out the foundation for a skyscraper, retaining walls are constructed to help keep the soil from sliding back into the freshly excavated pit.

Following excavation, foundations are poured for the underground substructure. A typical foundation consists of vertical columns that sit on top of spread footings, so that the loads from the building are transferred over relatively wide areas. Steel rebar (reinforcing bars) are set in place, concrete is poured, and the stage is set for the construction of the above-ground building to begin. First, the steel skeleton of the superstructure is created, and a curtain wall is eventually hung from this grid. This exterior cladding will not help support the weight of the structure; the steel cage and functional core bear the entire burden. Cladding is typically made of metal, stone, or glass, and is anchored or hung directly from the building's steel frame.

In addition to the structural pieces, the components that allow a building to sustain human life, such as heating and cooling systems, are crucial parts of the design and building process. Elevators are also fundamental to these structures. Elevator shafts are typically made of concrete that is poured over steel reinforcing bars. Horizontal living and working spaces within the giant vertical structure are created by placement of horizontal steel beams. Steel decking is typically welded to these beams, and floor slabs are poured on top.

Water pumps and sprinkler systems are added toward the end of the construction process. The final touch on the overall exterior of a building is the roof. A skyscraper's roof may be an architecturally designed showpiece, or it may be a simple floor-like system capped with waterproof roofing materials.

The last step in the construction of a skyscraper is usually interior finishing. While perhaps minor in comparison to the monumental construction effort required to build the exterior, the interior design is important because it should be pleasing to the building's occupants. First, interior wall and ceiling panels are put in place. Plumbing, electrical, and telephone lines are run throughout the building, and eventually lighting fixtures, bathroom equipment, and other utilities are installed. If the skyscraper has an observation or

The World Trade Center twin towers in New York, shown here under construction in 1970, broke records for height and available floor space.

viewing deck, the details of this feature are implemented around the same time. Then, finally, the building is ready to be inhabited, and its interior spaces can be furnished as desired as homes and offices.

SKYSCRAPERS' TENANTS

Skyscrapers are objects of beauty, but unlike art, they must be functional as well as aesthetic creations. Early skyscrapers were generally intended for use as commercial space, but today's skyscrapers tend to be more varied in their uses.

Many skyscrapers, both early and modern, have been built solely as places of business. The Home Insurance Company Building of 1885, for example, was essentially an office building. The Bank of China Tower in Hong Kong is a modern, triangular structure that rises to 1,209 feet (370 meters). New York's Empire State Building is home to 180 different companies, including real estate and public relations firms. Other skyscrapers are residences. Some of the most beautiful early skyscrapers were hotels, such as the Hotel Pierre, built in 1929, and the Sherry-Netherlands Hotel of 1927, two of the most easily recognized buildings in the New York skyline at the time.

Other skyscrapers have been built in homage to transportation. One example is the Midland Grand Hotel in London, built in 1873 as both a hotel and the terminus to a rail line. Prestige and image, in addition to profit, were major goals of this project.

In modern times, skyscrapers have even been built as symbols of a single individual. The Trump Tower in New York is a commemoration, of sorts, of its iconoclastic founder, Donald Trump. It is also one of the more expensive residential skyscrapers, consisting mainly of condominiums and penthouses.

THE START OF IT ALL

If the quest for tall, grandiose human-built structures began with the great pyramids of ancient Egypt, it took a different form in the modern age. The

Early skyscrapers like the Hotel Pierre reflected the elegance and attention to design that was typical of New York architecture in the 1930s.

structure that most agree was the first in the so-called skyscraper movement was not a habitable building. In preparation for the Paris World's Fair of 1889, which commemorated the centenary of the French Revolution, Gustave Eiffel submitted a groundbreaking design in a competition for an entranceway to the exposition.

Chosen as the winning entry, Eiffel's structure on the Champ de Mars is made of exposed iron, stands 985 feet (300 meters) tall, and weighs nearly 7,000 tons (6,350 metric tons). It contains an astonishing 2.5 million rivets and required hundreds of ironworkers to construct. It was the tallest building in the world until the United States began building skyscrapers in earnest; New York's Chrysler Building topped Eiffel's masterpiece in the 1930s.

The Eiffel Tower nearly did not survive to create a legacy, though. While many people embrace high-flying buildings, there is always a constituency that rails against them, often in full-blown rage. Many people considered the Eiffel Tower an eyesore. Some even called for its dismantling immediately following the exposition. The tower was saved in 1909, not for any aesthetic considerations but for purely practical reasons. Its 24-foot (7-meter) antenna proved useful in the growing field of communication. Interestingly, Paris's tallest structure today is the Allouis longwave transmitter, the central transmitter for all of France. Time has a way of creating monumentality even in the eyes of disbelievers, though, and today Paris cannot be imagined without its signature landmark.

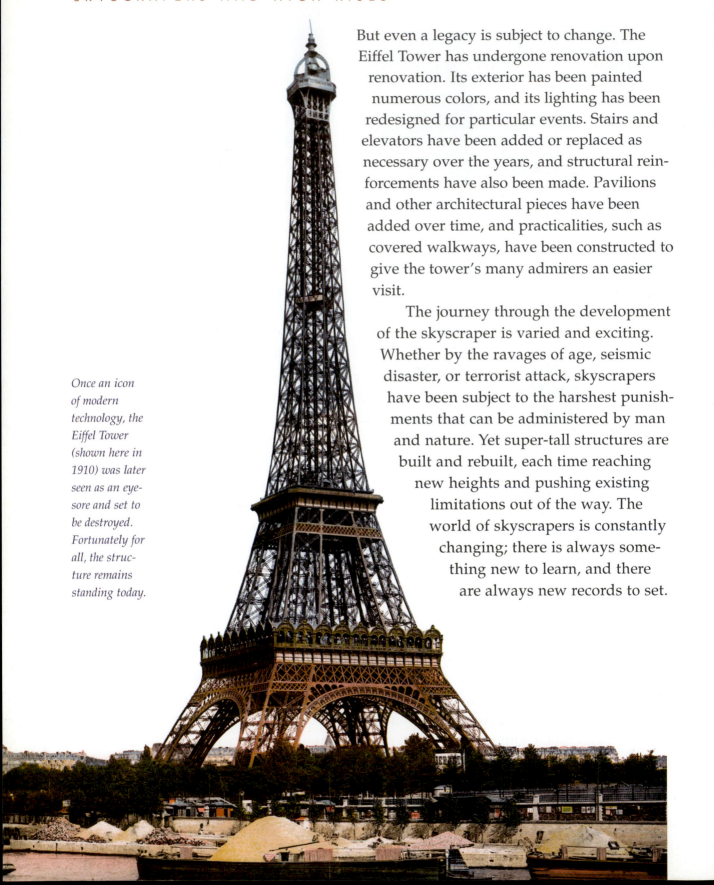

Once an icon of modern technology, the Eiffel Tower (shown here in 1910) was later seen as an eyesore and set to be destroyed. Fortunately for all, the structure remains standing today.

But even a legacy is subject to change. The Eiffel Tower has undergone renovation upon renovation. Its exterior has been painted numerous colors, and its lighting has been redesigned for particular events. Stairs and elevators have been added or replaced as necessary over the years, and structural reinforcements have also been made. Pavilions and other architectural pieces have been added over time, and practicalities, such as covered walkways, have been constructed to give the tower's many admirers an easier visit.

The journey through the development of the skyscraper is varied and exciting. Whether by the ravages of age, seismic disaster, or terrorist attack, skyscrapers have been subject to the harshest punishments that can be administered by man and nature. Yet super-tall structures are built and rebuilt, each time reaching new heights and pushing existing limitations out of the way. The world of skyscrapers is constantly changing; there is always something new to learn, and there are always new records to set.

SKYSCRAPER STYLE TIMELINE

Early Skyscrapers (1870s–1900s)
Tribune Building (1873)
Home Insurance Building (1885)
Tacoma Building (1889)
New York World Building (1890)

Chicago School (1880s–early 1900s)
Reliance Building (1895)
Monadnock Building (1891)
Wainwright Building (1891)

Early Modern (1900–1930s)
Flatiron Building (1902)
Woolworth Building (1913)
Hallidie Building (1918)

Art Deco (1920s-1930s)
Sherry-Netherlands Hotel (1927)
New York Life Insurance Company
   Building (1927)
Waldorf Astoria Hotel (1929)
Chrysler Building (1930)
Empire State Building (1930)

Modern (1920s–1950s)
Wrigley Building (1921)
Standard Oil Building (1926)
RCA Building (1928)

International Style (1930s–1970s)
CBS Building (1961)
New York Telephone Company Building
   (1967)
General Motors Building (1967)

Post-Modern (1970s +)
Citicorp Center (1974)
Trump Tower (1979)
Sony Building (1984)

Super-Tall (1970s +)
World Trade Center (1973)
Sears Tower (1973)
CN Tower (1976)
Petronas Twin Towers (1998)
Taipei 101 Tower (2004)

STRUCTURAL STEEL

Without steel, the skyscraper as we know it today would probably never have been developed. Steel and other technologies, such as the glass curtain wall and the elevator, are responsible for allowing engineers to design and build to soaring new heights. Steel possesses material properties that make it a particularly strong choice for skyscrapers. Architects took full advantage of the structural possibilities presented by steel, creating cities full of new landmarks.

BESSEMER AND THE MASS PRODUCTION OF STEEL

Engineers were familiar with steel as a building material in the mid-nineteenth century, but its possibilities were not fully realized until later. The turning point came in the 1880s with the creation of a process that manufactured steel quickly and inexpensively. As a result, steel became the material of choice for the construction of everything from bridges to skyscrapers.

The Flatiron Building's distinctive shape is as eye-catching today as it was in 1902.

Steel has roots in cast iron, an iron alloy that contains between 1.8 and 4.5 percent carbon. It also contains small percentages of silicon and manganese. The term cast iron comes from the fact that the iron alloy is cast into a shape specified by the designer for a particular use. Iron ore is melted in a blast furnace, cast into ingots, and allowed to set. It is then remelted along with other bits of scrap metal and shaped into its final form. Structurally, cast iron is very strong in compression but not in tension, which means that it can be used for load-bearing members but cannot generally be cast into tension wires.

In the 1880s, English inventor and engineer Henry Bessemer created a system to mass-produce a new material, steel, from molten iron. His system, called the Bessemer process, made cast iron more flexible by essentially removing the carbon from it. The process takes place in large containers known as Bessemer converters, which contain the molten iron as oxygen is blown through it. The resulting chemical reaction causes some of the carbon and other impurities to be burned off. The steel is then poured out and molded into its final shape. Modern steel production uses a variety of similar methods that are based on the Bessemer process but allow greater control of the chemical reaction and the exact chemical makeup of the final product.

Steel is a metal alloy composed of iron with a small percentage (0.02 to 1.5 percent) of carbon. While too much carbon makes steel and cast iron stiff and brittle, just the right amount makes it flexible yet very strong.

Steel is created through the Bessemer process. Shown here is a Bessemer converter at the Birmingham Steel Company.

Steel quickly became a very popular building material. It was inexpensive to produce in large batches, could be molded into whatever shape was required for a particular job, and could be bolted and welded together with more steel to create very tall structures. Its combination of strength and flexibility made it appropriate for many different uses, and a variety of basic shapes were developed for steel beams.

STEEL SECTIONS

Steel beams come in a variety of types that are identified by the letter formed by their cross-section. The W-type, or wide flange, beam has a cross-section that resembles an H. This is one of the most common structural steel sections, used primarily for load-bearing beams or columns. The W-type has thicker webs and flanges than other sections. The S-type, or American standard I-beam, is similar to a wide flange, but with sloping interior edges and a shorter flange length. C-types, or American standard channels, are sloped like an I-beam but shaped like a C, or approximately half of an I-beam.

C-types are not typically used as beams and columns because they lack sufficient structural strength. They are, however, used either as part of a composite beam welded together with other steel members, or in situations where part of a beam must have a straight edge to fit correctly into the structure; the solid back of the C-type provides this straight edge and makes it a very flexible steel section type.

How do engineers determine the length or strength of the steel beams they use? Steel sections are identified by their depth and weight. A wide

Steel sections come in different cross-sections, and each section has a specific construction usage.

 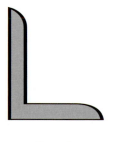 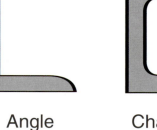  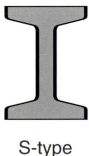 

S-type   W-type   Angle   Channel

MEASURING MATERIALS

A "lineal foot" is the standard means of measuring the dimensions of lumber, steel, or anything else that tends to come in long lengths. Lineal foot measures the length of such an object regardless of its weight, depth, or other dimensions. The engineer who designs the structural components of a building communicates the lineal foot measurements to the contractor, who is then responsible for its construction. A board that measures 2 inches x 4 inches x 12 feet (5 centimeters x 10 centimeters x 3.6 meters) is 12 lineal feet (3.6 lineal meters). Another board with dimensions of 3 inches x 6 inches x 12 feet (8 centimeters x 16 centimeters x 3.6 centimeters) also measures 12 lineal feet (3.6 lineal meters). Materials are also sometimes priced by the lineal foot. Disregarding the length for a moment, a thicker, wider board would most likely cost more per lineal foot than a narrower one.

flange denoted as a W10 x 30, for example, has a web 10 inches (25 centimeters) deep and a weight of 30 pounds per lineal foot (45 kilograms per lineal meter). Suppose this beam is 10 feet (3 meters) long. To calculate the actual weight of this beam, the weight per foot would be multiplied by the length. For example, 30 pounds per lineal foot times 10 feet equals 300 pounds. Once the weight that is to be supported has been determined, the appropriate beams can be chosen.

COLLABORATIVE STRUCTURE WITH REINFORCED CONCRETE

While steel is a useful building material on its own, it becomes even more so when combined with concrete. These two materials can be used together to create reinforced concrete, or concrete embedded with steel rods. While it may not sound like a huge technological advance, reinforced concrete is actually one of the most versatile building materials ever designed. Developed in mid–nineteenth-century France for domestic use, it was first used on a grand scale by the railroad industry.

Why must concrete be reinforced? Concrete is made by mixing gravel or some other aggregate and cement, forming a lattice structure. As a result, it can withstand considerable compressive forces but will crack when placed in tension. Consider a typical wooden lattice garden fence. The fence can easily support a few rocks leaned against it, which would exert a squeezing force. Pulling the fence between enormous vice grips, though, would cause it to stretch and then quickly break apart because the structure of the lattice cannot withstand stretching. Concrete, because of its lattice structure, has the same response. The internal structure is strong and compact, and resists being squeezed, but it can easily be pulled apart.

Therefore, any concrete structure that will have to resist tension forces must be reinforced with a material that can withstand tension, such as steel. Concrete reinforced with steel can be used in many construction situations because it can withstand both types of forces and can be molded into nearly any shape.

In the manufacture of reinforced concrete, steel reinforcing rods are sanded or molded with ridges so that the concrete poured over them will adhere completely. Once the concrete has been poured and is dry, the rods are permanently fixed within it. All materials expand and contract over time, depending on weather and other conditions. Concrete and steel have similar thermal expansion characteristics and tend to

Reinforced beams deflect significantly less than unreinforced beams, when subjected to equal loading conditions.

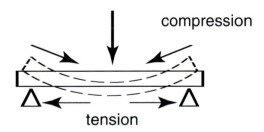

unreinforced: shows deflection

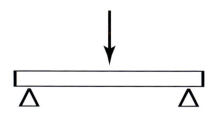

reinforced: minimal deflection

Reinforced concrete is created by pouring concrete around a web, or cage, of steel reinforcing bars.

shrink and expand at similar rates, making them highly compatible components.

An additional benefit to the steel in reinforced concrete is that the lime in the concrete helps to prevent corrosion, but the reinforcing bars must be properly adhered to the concrete or the steel will corrode due to exposure to air. Therefore, if reinforced concrete is not manufactured properly, corrosion can cause the concrete to crack.

The development of steel and reinforced concrete at the end of the nineteenth century provided the materials necessary for the construction of buildings that were taller than ever before. All that was needed was a place to use them. Unfortunately, one of the most devastating tragedies in American history provided the location.

THE GREAT CHICAGO FIRE OF 1871

It is often said that, throughout history, invention and success spring forth from the ruins of disaster. This was never truer than in the urban development that followed the fire that engulfed the city of Chicago in 1871. The nearly total destruction of the city led to a boom in steel production and building construction, which led to an increase in the development of skyscrapers.

Chicago in the 1870s was a town built largely of closely spaced wooden buildings. The area was suffering from a drought when, as legend has it, Catherine O'Leary's cow kicked over a candle in the barn. A fire ensued and spread rapidly throughout the city. The fire crossed the Chicago River and burned for a full day, destroying nearly four square miles of town

Decimated by the Great Fire of 1871, the city of Chicago had to undertake a tremendous cleanup effort before rebuilding could begin.

before rain showers finally helped firefighters gain an advantage over the wind-swept flames.

While the loss of human life was moderate—there were approximately 300 casualties—more than 18,000 buildings burned to the ground. The fire did not discriminate; it destroyed houses, hotels, department stores, and theaters—nearly everything in its path. The town's famous cast-iron buildings melted in the flames. One of the few surviving structures, the Chicago Water Tower, was built of limestone.

While Chicago is well known for this devastating fire, it is equally recognized for the speed at which the town was rebuilt. Almost immediately after the flames died down, citizens and business owners began sweeping the debris into the lake (which, by the way, eventually created landfill for new building projects). New ordinances (laws) were put in place for construction, including the requirement that buildings be able to withstand a fire for three hours before burning down. The city was rebuilt at an astounding pace and, by 1880, was a bustling boomtown.

Before the fire, one of Chicago's tallest buildings was the eight-story Palmer House Hotel owned by real estate developer Potter Palmer. The hotel was quickly rebuilt, and Palmer claimed that it was the "world's first fireproof building." The hotel was constructed largely of cast iron and brick, which, while not completely fireproof, certainly can withstand flames for longer than any wooden structure.

THE CHICAGO SCHOOL OF ARCHITECTURE, 1880–1900

The rapid rebuilding of Chicago led to an influx of all sorts of talented individuals. By 1890, Chicago was the second-largest U.S. city, and up-and-coming architects flocked to the area in droves. William Le Baron Jenney, Louis Sullivan, Frederick Baumann, and Dankmar Adler were some of the most important architects to contribute to what became known as the Chicago style, or Chicago School, of architecture. While their early designs in the 1870s and 1880s still focused on brick load-bearing walls, the use of steel skeleton frames was just around the corner.

Constructed in Chicago in 1885, the Home Insurance Building represented an impressive usage of steel framing.

Jenney was perhaps the foremost architect of this period, and many other great architects spent part of their early careers as apprentices at his firm. Jenney's major contribution was the Home Insurance Company Building, which he had originally specified as a load-bearing iron structure. The Carnegie Steel Company realized it could do the project in steel instead, resulting in the construction of one of the first skyscrapers.

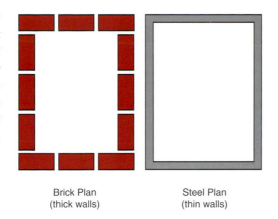

As seen in plan view, a brick skyscraper had to have thicker foundation walls than a steel-framed skyscraper.

Brick Plan
(thick walls)

Steel Plan
(thin walls)

There were several reasons that steel was preferable to iron. For starters, the building was essentially fireproof—an important consideration in a city recently devastated by fire. Furthermore, because the steel structure supported the weight of the building, only thin exterior cladding was needed, meaning more of the building could be used for retail space. This was important because in a typical brick building, the footprint of the building was diminished by the heavy, thick walls that were required to support the upper floors of the structure. Thicker walls meant less interior space for storeowners to display their merchandise. Steel construction made super-thick walls a thing of the past.

Also, steel weighed less than one-third of masonry materials, meaning Jenney's structure could be built higher than any other in the city before the weight of the building made it unstable. The modest ten-story Home Insurance Company Building does not seem at all remarkable today, but it showed architects what was possible when steel was used as a building material, and thereby started a race for increasingly tall buildings.

The Wainwright Building is often called a "crossover skyscraper" because it combined a steel frame with brick cladding.

Another important figure in the Chicago School was Louis Sullivan. Sullivan first came to Chicago after the Great Fire and worked in Jenney's office for a year before going to study in Paris. After returning to Chicago, he eventually obtained a job with Dankmar Adler's architectural firm. It was during this time that Sullivan made his first major contributions to skyscraper design.

Sullivan designed several ten-story steel skyscrapers. The Wainwright Building, built in St. Louis, Missouri, in 1891, relied entirely on a steel frame and made extensive use of ornamentation on the upper floors to contribute to the overall elegance of the building. Sullivan's motto when it came to skyscraper design was "Form follows function." For Sullivan, the physical shape of a building should respect its function, which, in the case of skyscrapers, was largely to provide office and retail space. The form of a steel skyscraper, because of its newfound height, was slim and vertical. This represented a significant contrast to previous large buildings, which were short and squat.

Skyscrapers could have larger windows than had been possible with the previous thick masonry construction, yet they lacked an overall aesthetic. Sullivan created the style used by many other architects in their skyscraper designs: a clean two-level base, an ornamented tall rise, and a cap at the roof level. This came to be "the look" for early twentieth-century skyscrapers.

THE FLATIRON BUILDING

Chicago was not the only city to have skyscrapers. In fact, skyscraper construction soon became a competition between America's cities. One of New York's first skyscrapers was the 1902 Flatiron Building. The building's official name was the Fuller Building, but once everyone recognized the building's resemblance to an old-fashioned flatiron, the nickname stuck.

The twenty-two–story building was designed by two Chicago architects, Daniel Burnham and John Root. Situated on a triangular swath of land in Manhattan, it reached a soaring height of 285 feet (86 meters). Structurally, the building consisted of a steel-frame skeleton clad with terra-cotta and limestone. It used the same basic three-part design of a Sullivan skyscraper. Burnham and Root added ornamentation as part of their own signature style, which was based on detailing from the French and Italian Renaissance. The panels covering the sides of the steel frame were extruded to varying depths, making the building look both active and impressive when seen from below.

What was life like in 1902 for early occupants of the Flatiron Building? The U.S. economy was strong at the time and businesses were booming. While many people did not own cars or have indoor plumbing or electricity in their homes, there was a general feeling that one day soon, these things would be available to everyone. New inventions were everywhere. Light bulbs and phonographs made indoor life more enjoyable, bridges and skyscrapers allowed more people to work in the city than ever before, and paved roads were just beginning to appear as automobile production stepped up. It was a time of innovation in architecture as well as in other products that improved everyday life.

Clearly, the invention of structural steel had enormous consequences for skyscraper development. It was the single most important event in the history of this developing building typology! However, as buildings grew ever taller, new problems arose. How would very tall buildings be navigated and occupied? How would people working on the first floor communicate with their counterparts on the one-hundredth floor? Chapter 3 examines some very important inventions, namely the elevator and the telephone, which made skyscrapers not only viable, but also livable.

New York's Flatiron Building is also known as the Fuller Building, and broke records for skyscraper height when construction was completed in 1902.

ART DECO SKYSCRAPERS

Some of the most prominent and memorable skyscrapers built in the early twentieth century were designed in the Art Deco style. This movement in the decorative arts and architecture originated in Western Europe and became a major style there and in the United States in the 1930s. The name Art Deco, which was applied to this period about twenty years after it ended, came from the 1925 Exposition Internationale des Arts Décoratifs et Industriels Modernes in Paris, where the style was first displayed. The style has been applied to everything from jewelry to furniture.

Art Deco was seen as a modern take on past styles. This modernism was reflected in all aspects of society. At that time, women gained rights and independence and were encouraged to take factory jobs while the men were off fighting the world wars. Artistically, new patterns and shapes emerged. Sharp angles, floral patterns, flashy metallic surfaces, and exaggerated forms were a few of the characteristics typical of Art Deco style.

New York's Art Deco Skyscrapers

As it was expressed in skyscraper design, Art Deco led to more ornamented buildings with elaborate tops. Shiny metals were used on the skyscrapers' upper levels, making these tall buildings true beacons in the sky. Two of the best-known Art Deco skyscrapers are the Chrysler Building (New York, 1930) and the Empire State Building (New York, 1930).

The Chrysler Building features a striking metallic cap with stepped chevrons. This building represents one of the first major uses of stainless steel in skyscraper construction, and it is ornamented at the upper levels with Chrysler car motifs such as eagle hood ornaments, gears, and hubcaps, which are placed at various locations. The Empire State Building also uses a tiered stepping pattern at the upper levels, though in this case the pattern is rectangular.

Rockefeller Center is another famous example of Art Deco design in

Rockefeller Center (New York, 1940) has elaborate sculptural decoration, with many original works of art inside the building.

New York City skyscraper history. This complex of nearly twenty buildings, funded by the Rockefellers in an urban renewal effort, includes some of New York's best-known buildings, such as Radio City Music Hall and the RCA Building (now the GE building). Art Deco hallmarks include bronze gilding, extensive use of exterior stainless steel, and highly stylized sculptural exteriors.

Art Deco in Chicago

While New York City was the birthplace of the Art Deco skyscraper, other cities began to produce their own modernistic buildings. The highly ornamented Chicago Board of Trade Building was designed by the architectural firm Holabird and Root and is one of Chicago's oldest Art Deco skyscrapers. The building has copious amounts of nonorthogonal geometry (geometry that does not strictly adhere to horizontal-vertical X-Y axes) that make for a very exciting facade. It uses sculptures in the building's details and has a double-height interior lobby typical of the period.

Another example of Art Deco in Chicago is the Palmolive Building, designed by Holabird and Root and constructed from 1927 to 1929. The design included the typical Art Deco facade with a stair-step configuration. Unlike the Empire State Building with its horizontal setbacks, the Palmolive Building uses both horizontal and vertical setbacks, which give it a very active appearance. This style was copied by many architects of Art Deco skyscrapers.

The Art Deco movement spawned the design of buildings with incredible attention to ornamentation, both inside and outside.

Other Architectural Examples

The Art Deco architectural style applied to more than just skyscrapers. One of the best-known Art Deco buildings in the world is located in Rotterdam, the Netherlands. Designed by architect J.J.P. Oud in 1930, the Kiefhook Housing estate is an early modern housing complex that incorporates characteristics of the Art Deco style. Its brick structure, covered in plaster for a smooth white appearance, has the clean lines typical of modern architecture, but a more ornamented exterior.

3

ELEVATORS AND COMMUNICATIONS

Steel allowed engineers to design increasingly tall buildings, and the elevator made them habitable by humans. The telephone made communication between floors simple. Building technology was responsible for the rapid growth and popularity of high-rise buildings, but the buildings would have been largely useless without these other important inventions.

ELEVATORS

Basic devices for lifting people or objects have existed for nearly 2,000 years. Ancient Greeks, for example, developed manually powered hoists for use in constructing temples. Centuries later, more advanced hoists were developed to move cartons around in factories. Steam-powered and hydraulic elevators were invented in the early nineteenth century for use primarily in mines and factories.

One of the most fascinating aspects of the Chrysler Building is the ornamentation and detail of the interior spaces.

OTIS AND THE DEVELOPMENT OF THE ELEVATOR

Elisha Otis (1811–1861), while not the inventor of the elevator, was the man largely responsible for its success through his invention of a critical safety feature: the modern elevator brake. Otis was raised on a farm in Vermont and later opened a factory in New York, the nineteenth-century Mecca for industry and innovation. In his early years Otis experimented with designing hoisting cars for lifting heavy objects, but his major contribution came after a fatal elevator accident in his New York factory. He developed a mechanical device to maintain the stability of the elevator car in the event of a cable failure, one that (for the first time) did not rely on the elevator operator. His invention proved to be a lifesaver, literally, and became the basis for modern elevator mechanics.

Dubbed the founder of the modern elevator, Elisha Graves Otis made the elevator more reliable with his invention of the safety brake.

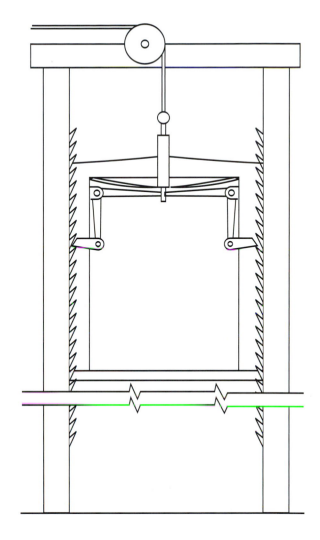

The Otis safety brake made elevator usage much more reliable for tall skyscrapers.

The turning point in elevator design came in 1852, when Elisha Graves Otis developed what he called the safety elevator. Otis's design used what was then the standard elevator car and ropes, but incorporated a braking device that locked the car in place should the hoisting ropes fail. For the first time, people could feel safe traveling in elevators.

HYDRAULIC ELEVATORS

The earliest types of elevators were hydraulic, meaning that they involved some sort of fluid and a pump. In the simplest type of hydraulic elevator, a piston is mounted in a cylinder. The piston, which is simply a rod that can move up and down, is attached to the bottom of the elevator. The cylinder is filled with an incompressible fluid, such as oil, and extra fluid is stored in a tank attached to the cylinder with pipes. The system also has a pump and a series of valves.

To make the elevator rise, the valve is opened and oil is pumped into the cylinder. As the pressure in the cylinder increases, the piston is forced up as the bottom of the cylinder fills with oil. Since the piston is attached to the bottom of the elevator car, the elevator and its passengers move up as well.

More modern hydraulic elevator cars, used mainly in buildings a few stories in height, contain a system for passengers to tell the elevator at

Hydraulic elevators use a pump system, combined with a large piston, to raise and lower the elevator car.

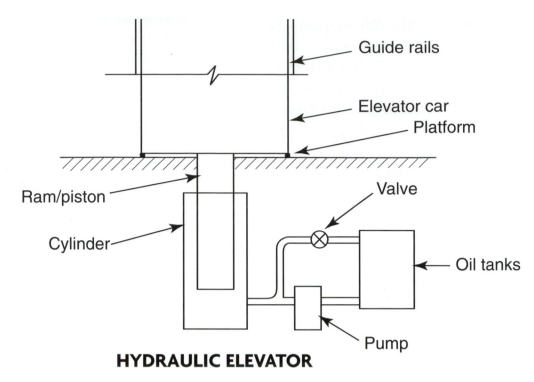

Guide rails

Elevator car

Platform

Ram/piston

Cylinder

Valve

Oil tanks

Pump

HYDRAULIC ELEVATOR

which floor they would like to stop. Passengers push a button indicating a floor, and an electrical signal is sent to the motor. Once the elevator reaches the desired floor, the valve is closed and the pump stops adding fluid to the cylinder. With the valve closed, however, the fluid that is already in the cylinder is stuck there, and the pressure of the fluid continues to support the piston in its vertical position, countering the force of gravity.

To make the elevator descend, the valve is opened and fluid slowly flows back into the tank. As the cylinder empties, the piston travels down in the cylinder under the force of gravity. Once the elevator reaches the desired floor, the valve is again closed. Since the hydraulic system is completely self-contained, no fluid is lost as the elevator travels up and down, and the process can be carried out repeatedly.

The main disadvantage of hydraulic elevators is that the piston and cylinder must extend to the top of the building. Since the piston is a rigid object, the cylinder must in fact be twice as tall as the building. A five-story building would require a ten-story cylinder extending from five stories underground to five stories above the ground to accommodate the piston at both the top and bottom floors. To get around this disadvantage, a new elevator was designed that required less space and was more efficient: the cable elevator.

CABLE ELEVATORS

Another popular type of elevator is a rope-based, or cable, elevator. As opposed to a hydraulic system, where the car is literally pushed up, a cable elevator uses braided steel cables and a motor to raise or lower the car. The elevator car is attached to the cables, which loop around a pulley in a mechanical room situated near the top of the building directly over the elevator shaft. The pulley is driven by a motor that runs in two directions, one to raise the cables and the other to lower them.

In order to reduce the amount of energy required by the motor and cables, elevators make use of a counterweight. This is a large weight equal to the weight of the car plus about 40 percent of the maximum passenger load. The counterweight is attached to the cables on the other side of the pulley. When the car begins to go up or down, part of the load is balanced by this counterweight, so the motor has less work to do. The amount of potential energy in the elevator system therefore remains consistent, which means a longer life for all of the elevator's components as well as less power required by the motor.

In physics, work (W) is defined as the transfer of energy from one object to another, and is a combination of force (F) and distance (D):

$$W = F \times D$$

Imagine a box that is being pushed along the floor. The work required to move the

Cable elevators were also called rope or pulley elevators, and were more expensive to install than hydraulic elevators. They were, however, much more practical for very tall buildings.

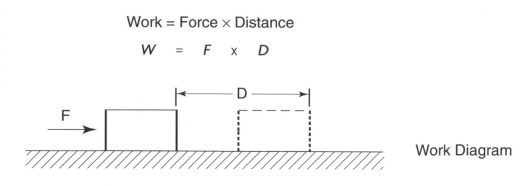

Work = Force × Distance

$$W = F \times D$$

Work Diagram

The amount of work required to move an object is equal to the force pushing that object, multiplied by the distance the object is being moved.

box is the force (the amount of effort it takes to move the box) times the distance the box moves.

In the case of an elevator, the amount of work done by the motor is conceptually equal to the force applied to it by the elevator multiplied by the distance of the ropes the motor is moving. The amount of force applied is

NEWTON'S THIRD LAW

Newton's third law of motion states that all actions have an equal and opposite reaction. In the absence of movement, any object that exerts a force upon another is reacted upon by that same amount of force. Imagine a brick that is placed on a table. Assuming that the brick does not fall through the table, gravity exerts a downward force on the mass of the brick, causing it to press down on the table. This force is equal to the force that the table exerts upon the brick to support it. An elevator stopped between two floors provides a good conceptual example of Newton's third law. The force of the cable pulling up on the elevator equals the force of gravity pulling down on the elevator, which is the weight of the car itself and the people inside it. Because these forces are balanced, the car is at rest.

greatly reduced by the addition of the counterweight; therefore, the amount of work the motor must perform is also reduced.

The counterweight works to preserve the potential energy of the elevator system. If the counterweight and the elevator car were perfectly balanced, as would be the case when the elevator car was filled to 40 percent of capacity, then the system would require just a tiny amount of energy to move the elevator up or down. When the elevator car moves down, it loses potential energy, and the counterweight on the other side of the cable moves up, gaining potential energy. That potential energy can then be utilized the next time the elevator car needs to move up—as the counterweight moves down, the elevator car moves up. Potential energy is again transferred, and little force, and therefore little work, is required by the motor.

ELEVATOR SAFETY

Hydraulic elevators have a safety system provided by the piston. No complicated braking device was needed, since the piston provided the necessary support for the car. Cable elevators are just as safe, though conceptually a little trickier to understand. The cable systems are redundant, meaning that several more cables than are actually needed are designed into each elevator. If one cable were to rupture, other cables would carry the load. If all the cables were to break simultaneously, safety brakes, such as those developed by Elisha Otis, would maintain the safety of the car and its passengers.

Otis sold his first elevator featuring the safety brake in 1853. It was used to haul freight, not passengers. In 1854, Otis dramatically demonstrated the elevator safety brake at the World's Fair of the Works of Industry of All Nations in New York. He rode up to a good height and ordered the cable to be cut.

THE FIRST PASSENGER ELEVATOR

A few years after the invention of the safety brake, Otis's elevator was purchased for use in the E.V. Haughwout and Company department store

Built in New York in 1857, the Haughwout Building is a cast-iron structure that was designed to look like a Venetian library.

in New York City. The five-story cast-iron building, designed by John Gaynor, was built in 1857. Otis installed his elevator in this building, and for the first time customers could easily access higher floors for their shopping convenience. The expense of the elevator was easily balanced by the increase in traffic to the store, and the Otis Elevator Company came into high demand.

When Elisha Otis died in 1861, his sons took over the business, and it grew exponentially. Hotel owners were the first to fully embrace the passenger elevator. In the late nineteenth century, hotels were largely for the wealthy, and hotel owners were able to commission increasingly tall buildings that could be easily traversed.

An interesting side note is that the top floor of high-rise hotels had generally been given to the resident cleaning crews, since no one else wanted to walk up many flights of stairs each evening! Today, penthouse rooms and floors are some of the most desirable locations in hotels and apartment buildings.

Modern elevators use a variety of redundant safety techniques to ensure that passengers are protected in the case of an emergency. Systems of gears are engaged if the cables break and the elevator starts falling too quickly. These gears trigger the deployment of emergency brakes, which use a variety of techniques to slow the descent of a runaway elevator car and gradually bring it to a stop. If all else fails, a large shock absorber is present at the bottom of the elevator shaft to cushion the fall.

The skyscrapers of today rely on elevators to transport occupants to their desired floors. Without elevators, it is doubtful that skyscrapers or other tall buildings would even exist. They do, however, come at something of a price. An elevator shaft must be constructed for each elevator or bank of elevators, and this takes up precious space. Designers must make up for this missing square footage somewhere else, often by adding more floors.

Occupancy loads are another important consideration. Each elevator has a maximum capacity based on its size and method of construction. Small residential elevators, for example, may have a maximum load of 1,000 to 2,000 pounds (450 to 900 kilograms), while large freight elevators are able to carry many times that amount.

INVENTION OF THE TELEPHONE

With the advent of the elevator, all floors of very tall buildings could be occupied. This presented a communication problem, however. If a company occupied twenty floors in a high rise, employees on the first floor would

Telephones were a very important development for making skyscrapers usable. Without them, there would be no communication between floors!

THIS MODEL OF BELL'S FIRST TELEPHONE IS A DUPLICATE OF THE INSTRUMENT THROUGH WHICH SPEECH SOUNDS WERE FIRST TRANSMITTED ELECTRICALLY, 1875.

43

need to talk to employees on the twentieth floor. Early corporations hired messengers to run up and down the stairs, but this was an expensive practice with a large potential for messages to become lost or mistranslated. Another invention was needed to help communication within skyscrapers. That invention was the telephone.

While many individuals contributed to the science and design of the telephone, its first patent was issued to Alexander Graham Bell. He conducted many experiments with the same type of electrical signals that had gone into the development of the telegraph some thirty years earlier. The biggest problem with the telegraph was that only one message could be sent through a wire in one direction at a time.

Bell's first advance was the ability to send multiple messages simultaneously over the wire. Later he discovered a method for electrically transmitting speech through wire by varying the strength of the current running through the wire. The addition of a transmitter, which Bell also developed, resulted in the device that came to be known as the telephone.

TELEPHONE SCIENCE

Telephones work by transmitting sound waves. A person speaking creates sound waves, which enter the mouthpiece of the telephone. Behind the mouthpiece is a device called a transmitter, which vibrates like the human eardrum. The transmitter is similar to a microphone. In the case of a simple telephone, the transmitter consists of grains of carbon sandwiched between two thin metal plates. The sound waves from the person's voice

The mechanics of the telephone are such that when a person speaks into a receiver, sound waves are filtered and transmitted until they reach the receiver held by a second person.

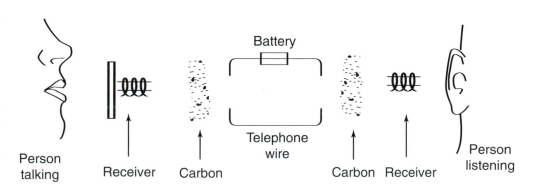

Person talking   Receiver   Carbon   Battery / Telephone wire   Carbon   Receiver   Person listening

SOUND WAVES

A sound wave is a pattern of air disturbance, caused by energy as it passes through air or some other medium away from the source of the sound. The speed at which a sound wave travels is defined as the distance the wave travels per unit of time: speed (wave) = distance/time.

The speed of sound waves traveling through air is about 767 miles per hour (343 meters per second). Note that sound waves do not always have to travel through air. Dolphins, for example, emit sounds that travel through the water and then bounce back. Sound waves travel quickly through water, at about 3,355 miles per hour (1,500 meters per second)—nearly five times the speed at which sound waves travel through air! The speed of a sound wave is relative to the density of the material through which it travels. Unlike light, which is an electromagnetic wave, sound waves cannot travel through a vacuum. While we receive light and other radiation from distant stars and galaxies, for example, we receive no sounds from them.

enter the mouthpiece, causing the metal plate to vibrate and compressing the grains of carbon.

The rapid compressing and decompressing of the carbon grains from the vibration actually change the resistance of the carbon, which alters the amount of electrical current that flows through the transmitter. It is this change, or modulation, in current that is sent down the telephone wires and then recreated at the other end as sound in the recipient's telephone. Modern telephones use an electronic microphone and circuit to encode and decode the voice of the person speaking, but the basic idea is still the same.

Telephones are plugged into a wall jack, allowing them to send electrical currents that transmit sound waves into the receiver of the other person's telephone. The receiver contains a diaphragm with two magnets; one holds the diaphragm in place, while the other is an electromagnet that controls how the diaphragm vibrates. When an electrical current enters the receiver and passes over the coil of the electromagnet, the diaphragm is pulled in to varying extents, depending on what the person at the other end of the conversation is saying. The diaphragm vibrates accordingly, and, as it does so, air is moved in front of it. This change in air pressure creates sound waves that are identical to the waves being produced in the transmitter. The person holding the receiver is sent these sound waves, which form the words being said by the person at the other end of the line.

BOON TO THE SKYSCRAPER INDUSTRY

In addition to the obvious workflow advantages of having telephone service inside a skyscraper, another major plus for the industry was the ability to communicate during construction. In the years before mobile telephone service became widely available, contractors often constructed temporary phone lines for use during the construction of a building. For the first time, workers on the hundredth floor could easily commu-

Without an understanding of sound waves, Alexander Graham Bell might never have arrived at the first working telephone prototype.

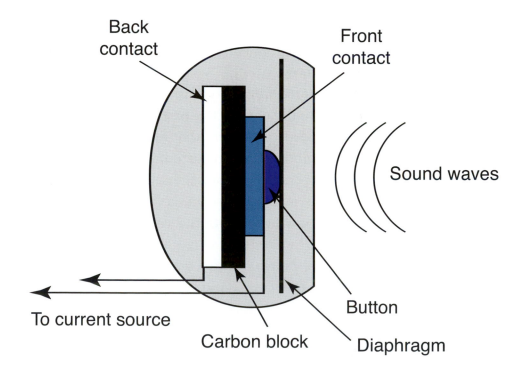

Back contact

Front contact

Sound waves

To current source

Carbon block

Button

Diaphragm

nicate with the architect on the ground, and parts could be brought up without a steel contractor having to take the time to descend. Once construction was completed, the temporary lines were removed and permanent telephone systems were installed. Recently, mobile telephone service has revolutionized the speed and efficiency with which large skyscrapers are built.

The development of skyscrapers and that of telephones were mutually beneficial. Skyscrapers were seen as a shining example of success for the telephone industry; they were essentially free advertising for the burgeoning field of communications. Once it became clear how successful and necessary telephones were to skyscrapers, the communications industry grew exponentially and came out with increasing numbers of innovations. Consider that a skyscraper was essentially a city unto itself; all the necessary services were contained inside a single building. In cities that were developing standardized telephone service, telephone poles for stringing wires were becoming commonplace. In a skyscraper, however, the phone wires were hidden in the building's service core and invisible to the building's occupants. Telephones became ubiquitous as their increased usage (and more sophisticated building technology) led to their seemingly magical appearance throughout buildings.

While the technological achievement of building a skyscraper was certainly newsworthy, it was the amenities such as elevators and telephones that allowed the skyscraper to be used for its intended purpose. From Elisha Otis to Alexander Graham Bell, inventors paved the way for skyscraper interiors to function as well as their structures did.

FACADES
AND FACING

Many buildings, whether they are exceptionally beautiful or truly horrendous, elicit a strong emotional response from those who see them. We are all taught not to judge a book by its cover. However, laypeople often evaluate architecture based on first impressions generated by the building's exterior. All buildings have some sort of exterior facing, or facade. This layer, often called cladding, is necessary for a building to be functional. There are two main considerations in determining what type of cladding should be applied—aesthetics and suitability.

One of the groundbreaking Art Deco skyscrapers is the Chrysler Building (New York, 1930).

If the building is to appear very austere, such as a bank's headquarters, granite or limestone cladding might be an appropriate choice. Or, if the architect is designing a monument to an important figure, a shiny homage of steel and glass would make sense. Energy efficiency is another important consideration; brick and stucco tend to be excellent insulators, while glass is less so. Stone, metal, and glass are all valid choices for skyscraper facades. Cladding materials can be used to create many different visual impressions, and each building material has properties that make it more or less suitable for a particular building.

MASONRY

Stone was the building material of choice for much of the architecture in prehistoric civilizations, such as the monoliths at Stonehenge. The ancient Egyptians used stone to build the pyramids, and later the Greeks and

The Monadnock Building of 1893 was actually Chicago's tallest sky-scraper—and the world's largest office building—at the time of its construction.

PHILADELPHIA CITY HALL

The city hall in Philadelphia, Pennsylvania, is an exception to the rule of maximum height for buildings constructed using load-bearing masonry. The world's tallest building of this type, Philadelphia City Hall reaches a soaring height of 548 feet (167 meters). Built between 1871 and 1901—yes, it really took thirty years!—the exterior walls are made of limestone, granite, and brick. At the base, these walls are about 22 feet (6.5 meters) thick, which is about the length of two small cars placed end to end.

Romans constructed numerous monuments and temples of this highly durable substance. Stone is one of several materials that are collectively called masonry. The term refers to anything constructed with materials used by masons. These skilled workers build structures by layering individual pieces of stone or brick.

Before steel was available as an affordable structural system for skyscrapers, early tall buildings were constructed entirely of brick. The original Monadnock Building, designed by Chicago architects Daniel H. Burnham and John Wellborn Root, was one of the last tall buildings in Chicago to use a time-tested structural technique in which the walls themselves supported the weight of the building. This technique used load-bearing masonry, which gave the building a traditional, almost regal feel. The construction of this type of building was highly labor-intensive. The walls had to be nearly 6 feet (2 meters) thick at the bottom in order to support the weight of the upper walls. The maximum height for this type of building was around 150 to 200 feet.

By the time architects had become successful at designing twenty-story buildings made of load-bearing masonry, the technique had been explored to its fullest. The world was due for a change. That change came in the form of steel. As steel became an affordable, strong, and flexible building alternative for skyscrapers, designers began creating steel-framed skyscrapers in earnest. In fact, the Monadnock Building acquired an addition in 1891 that used a steel-frame structural skeleton. This building is one of the only examples of such a structure, combining the last of the old construction methods with the first of the new.

CURTAIN WALLS

The strength and flexibility of steel allows building designers to support the loads of buildings with a much smaller frame. Rather than requiring massive walls of brick to support a building, a smaller steel skeleton bears the load of floors and walls. An outer layer of cladding protects the building's interior from the elements. A facade hung from a structural steel frame does not provide support for the building. The main load that it incurs is its own dead load, or the weight of its materials. These loads are partially transferred to the building through beams, girders, and the connectors upon which the facade rests. Such cladding is often attached to steel brackets, which in turn are welded to the steel girders of the floor frames. This type of facade, called a curtain wall, was used extensively once steel framing became more common. Curtain walls can be made from masonry, metal, or glass.

A curtain-wall facade performs a number of important duties. Aside from keeping out the rain and cold air, a facade must support several types of loads in addition to its own weight. Wind loads are a factor, since the facade is the building's only line of defense against the wind. The building must be designed to withstand some percentage above the maximum predicted wind load for that specific location. Similarly, snow loads could be a

This detail shows how curtain walls are hung off a steel frame.

consideration, but only if parts of the facade are slanted at more than a 15-degree angle; if there is less of a slant, snow will not tend to collect on the facade and will not contribute a sizable load to the overall building. In some parts of the world, seismic loads are a major design factor. When earthquakes are a possibility, a hanging curtain wall must have anchors and hangers designed to allow for flexibility and movement. In addition, the wall must be able to accommodate some amount of movement between the floors of the building.

BRICK CLADDING

One of the oldest surviving examples of an entirely brick-clad skyscraper is the Manhattan Building in Chicago. Designed by William Le Baron Jenney and built in 1891, this sixteen-story building was one of the first steel-framed structures to utilize clips, or hangers, from which the cladding was hung. The brick facade, heavier and more rusticated at the bottom than the top, was decorated with terra-cotta ornaments, which give the building an elegant feel.

Chicago's Manhattan Building was one of William Le Baron Jenney's crowning achievements. It was one of the first steel-framed skyscrapers with wide enough window bays to offer sufficiently lighted interiors.

Many skyscrapers that came out of the Chicago School of architecture used a steel frame with masonry cladding. A prime example is the 1894 Old Colony Building, designed by architects William Holabird and Martin Roche. The building was framed in steel and then enclosed with different types of masonry that were hung in large panels from the

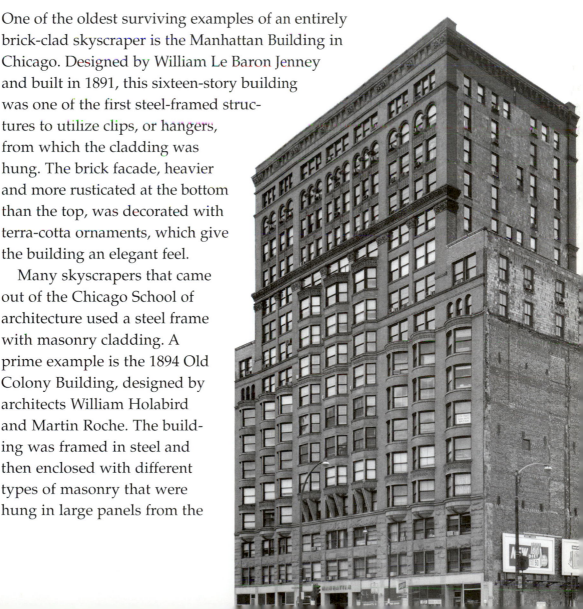

Another famous Chicago skyscraper is the Old Colony Building of 1894.

steel frame. A somewhat unusual structural twist to this building is that wrought-iron arches, aided by horizontal beams, actually support the floor.

Holabird and Roche used the cladding materials to create a facade in three sections. This assembly was designed to mimic the tripartite division of an ancient Greek column, which has a base, shaft, and capital. The Old Colony Building used limestone for the first several stories and the upper levels. In between, the rest of the building was faced with tan brick. Like other skyscrapers of the time, terra-cotta was used for ornamentation.

This building also made use of another innovation in skyscraper design—rounded corner windows. Not only did this design give the building a distinguished appearance, but also it allowed more light to reach the interior.

METAL

One of the first skyscraper designers to abandon the use of the heavy masonry facade was Ernest Flagg. For the Singer Tower, built in New York City in 1908, Flagg used a facade composed mainly of glass and iron lattice. Unfortunately, this early example of non-masonry cladding was

The impressive Singer Building (New York, 1908) unfortunately was demolished in 1968.

demolished to make room for a much larger skyscraper, the U.S. Steel Building, which opened in 1972. Now known as One Liberty Plaza, this building resides next to the former site of the World Trade Center towers.

The advent of stainless steel around 1910 presented architects and designers with a new material for skyscraper facades that had many advantages. Stainless steel, so called because of its perpetually shiny and rust-free appearance, is a high-grade steel with lower than normal carbon content. By definition, it contains at least 12 percent chromium. Stainless steel has particular physical and chemical properties that make it useful in many ways.

When exposed to oxygen, the chromium in stainless steel forms a layer of chromium oxide at the surface. This layer, which is too thin to be seen with the naked eye, gives stainless steel its shiny appearance. Interestingly, chromium oxide molecules are very close in size to simple chromium atoms, allowing the two substances to pack together closely at the surface in a long-lasting, protective coating. Iron also forms a protective oxide on its surface, but since the iron molecule is much smaller than the iron oxide, the two layers do not form a tight layer. The loose layer of oxidized iron flakes away as rust, causing iron to corrode quickly. This is one of the many reasons that steel quickly replaced cast iron as a building material.

STAINLESS STEEL

An interesting fact about stainless steel is that it exhibits a property called passivity; in other words, it is able to repair itself when scratched. When a piece of stainless steel is scratched, part of the chromium oxide layer is removed. This layer quickly regenerates itself due to a chemical reaction that occurs when chromium oxide is exposed to oxygen. The surface of the metal remains smooth and unmarred to the naked eye. However, stainless steel corrodes much more quickly in a non–oxygen-rich environment, such as under water, than it does when exposed to air.

Stainless steel is a superior cladding material because it is strong and flexible and does not rust. Because of this resistance to corrosion and other forms of staining, stainless steel is used for everything from kitchen cutlery to medical equipment.

A major example of stainless steel cladding is in New York City's Chrysler Building. Built between 1928 and 1930 in the Art Deco style, this masterpiece was designed by architect William Van Alen as the tallest building of its day (it was surpassed by the Empire State Building a year after construction was completed). While the lower parts of the facade were built using different-colored bricks, the cascading crescents at the top are clad in stainless steel. This was a noted first in skyscraper design, and the building quickly became a signature element in the New York City skyline.

The design for these unusual crescent shapes stemmed from a request by Walter P. Chrysler, who commissioned the building, that automobile icons be incorporated in the design. Van Alen attached eagle monuments at the corners of the building on the sixty-first floor that mimic the most popular hood ornament in the Chrysler Corporation's 1929 lineup.

The steel for the Chrysler Building was manufactured by a German company, Krupp, which was known for its cannons, ammunition, and other military supplies. Van Alen chose a stainless steel with 18 percent chromium, because the shiny chromium oxide layer would be able to replenish itself easily from reactions with oxygen in the atmosphere, remaining bright without requiring maintenance.

GLASS

In addition to masonry and metal, glass is a major component of any skyscraper's facade. Without it, these buildings would not be habitable. Occupants would have no source of natural light or means by which to observe the outside world.

Glass is created by melting silica sand at temperatures of at least 3,600 degrees Fahrenheit (1,982 degrees Celsius). Other materials, including soda ash and limestone, are often added. Soda ash lowers the melting temperature of sand to make it easier to heat, while lime increases the hardness. When made naturally, without any other additives, glass tends to look green because of the iron that is present in sand. To render the glass clear, lead oxide can be added during the melting process. Once the mixture is melted and cooled, it takes on the key property of glass, transparency.

The use of glass in buildings dates back to at least the eleventh century B.C.E. Medieval churches made use of glass windows, and stained glass was used extensively in Romanesque and Gothic cathedrals. At that time, glass was blown to form vases or other

Reaching to the sky but no longer topping the height chart, New York's Chrysler Building remains an example of innovative engineering coupled with decorative detail.

Any Chrysler product would not be complete without automotive ornamentation! This is demonstrated by the Chrystler Building's eagle motif outcroppings, located hundreds of feet in the air.

curved shapes, and then swung flat to make sheets of glass. A new technique was developed in 1902 for creating flat glass known as float glass. In this process, molten glass is floated in a pressurized tin bath and made into perfectly flat panes.

WHY IS GLASS TRANSPARENT?

This phenomenon is best explained using the concepts of liquid and solid. The molecules of a solid (such as wood or metal) are organized into a distinguishable structure, meaning that light cannot pass through them. The molecules that make up a liquid are fluid, without a rigid structure, so light can pass through parts of the liquid. Glass has characteristics of both a solid and a liquid, which makes it structurally firm like a solid, yet transparent like a liquid.

GLASS FACADES

One of the first glass curtain-wall skyscrapers was the 1918 Hallidie Building in San Francisco, designed by architect Willis Polk. What was unusual about this design was that the curtain wall contained mostly glass, separated by metal mullions. This was the first instance in which the primary material in a building facade was something other than masonry. A concrete sill was cantilevered out from the steel structure, and this sill supported the weight of the glass curtain wall. The inspiration for this glass facade came more from necessity than from the desire for fame. Polk had a limited budget for this building, and glass was the least expensive option available.

Many New York skyscrapers built in the 1970s and 1980s had facades of aluminum and glass. The design of 1166 Sixth Avenue, by the firm of Skidmore, Owings, and Merrill, and completed in 1973, obtained a sleek, professional aesthetic using black tinted glass for the facade. This was combined with alternating aluminum mullions to create a cohesive and modern look.

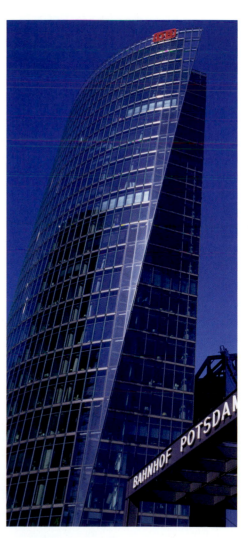

Whether masonry, glass, or some other material is used, skyscraper cladding is the building's first line of defense against the elements. Exterior facing works with the structure to provide an inhabitable building that can serve its intended purpose. However, without internal mechanical systems such as plumbing and heating, the building would not be very pleasant to occupy! Chapter 5 goes into the details of how these supplemental systems work and why they are an integral part of skyscraper design.

Although there is a variety of cladding materials available to skyscraper designers, glass is a desirable material because it gives the building such a striking appearance.

PETRONAS TWIN TOWERS

The other twin towers in the world of skyscrapers are the Petronas Twin Towers, located in Kuala Lumpur, Malaysia. Designed by New York architect Cesar Pelli, the towers were commissioned by Petronas, Malaysia's national petroleum company, and serve as its headquarters. Construction was completed on these 1,483-foot (452-meter) giants in 1998, and they were the world's tallest buildings until 2004.

Structurally, the Petronas Twin Towers were designed using a reinforced concrete core with exterior columns. Concrete is a heavy material, weighing approximately 4,000 pounds per cubic yard (2,373 kilograms per cubic meter). Because the buildings were so tall and heavy, they required foundations measuring more than 394 feet (120 meters) deep! More fire resistant than steel alone, reinforced concrete allows for very tall, thin buildings with a high resistance to wind and earthquakes.

The curtain-wall facades on these skyscrapers are a modernistic glass-and-steel combination, and the buildings are connected at the forty-first floor by a bridged enclosure. Because of its proximity to the equator, the light tends to be very bright in Kuala Lumpur. For this reason, most windows on these buildings are equipped with built-in sun shading. While most of the building is used as office space, the lower levels house a concert hall, shops, and public space. The basic outline of the skyscrapers is an eight-pointed star, which can be viewed largely by traversing the buildings' interiors or from a vantage point above. This shape, combined with ornamentation throughout the buildings, recalls early Islamic architecture. The building's owners wanted to express Malaysia's Muslim heritage, so Islamic shapes were incorporated into both the interior and exterior.

One of the more interesting asides about this project is that the two towers were built simultaneously by two different contractors. Tower One was built by the Hazama Corporation, while Tower Two was constructed by the Samsung Construction Company. The companies were set against each other in a race, and Tower Two won even though it was begun weeks after Tower One.

Kuala Lumpur's Petronas Towers were another pair of famous buildings that topped the height charts until Taipei 101 was completed. The plans are based on an eight-sided star design.

MECHANICAL AND ELECTRICAL SYSTEMS

The main purpose for the construction of any skyscraper is its use as living or working space. Many of the systems that are taken for granted by a building's inhabitants require painstaking planning and execution by designers, engineers, and contractors.

In today's modern digital environment, for example, it would be ridiculous to design a skyscraper without electricity or Internet connectivity. More basic systems, such as plumbing, sewage, and garbage removal, are equally if not more important. Skyscraper design has evolved over the years to allow for the inclusion of all these necessary services.

Skyscrapers under development can represent many different phases of the construction process, all at once.

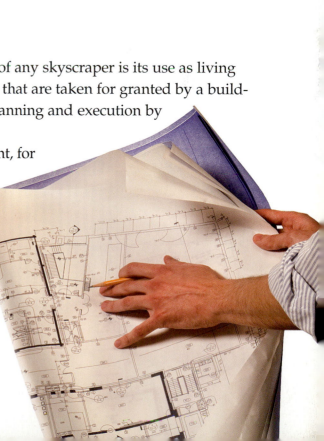

CORE AND SUPERSTRUCTURE

Most modern skyscrapers use a central core to house the mechanical equipment that keeps a building working. The building's floors are supported by beams that extend out from this core. The superstructure, which consists of windows, cladding, and other exterior building materials, is hung from these beams and exists as a separate system from the core.

Constructing the building's core and superstructure involves a specific, methodological process. A foundation hole is dug and steel piles are driven deep into the bedrock. Calculating the depth of a foundation depends on many factors, including the ultimate height of the skyscraper, the depth of the building's basement, and the amount of bedrock in the underlying soil. Often, reinforced concrete retaining walls are built into the foundation to keep the pit open, and to keep dirt from falling back into the hole.

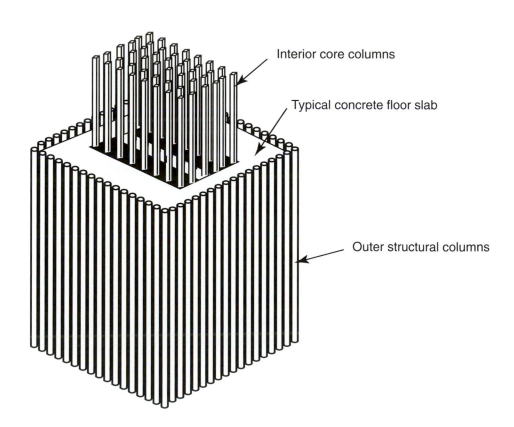

Interior core columns

Typical concrete floor slab

Outer structural columns

Many modern skyscrapers are designed using a structural exterior frame, with an interior core that acts as a separate system.

Reinforced skyscraper foundations are often constructed by pouring concrete over a steel cage.

A concrete foundation is then poured, and construction of the actual skyscraper can begin. First, vertical steel columns are erected, usually to a height of a few floors. At this point, floor beams are attached to the columns for those initial floors, and subflooring is laid so that contractors can safely walk through the building during construction. Then another few levels of vertical columns are constructed, followed by the addition of more floors.

A construction process called slip forming allows for on-site construction of a stable central core to house the mechanical equipment. Wood frames for a concrete wall are attached to the steel frame, a steel-reinforcing cage is inserted into the framework, and concrete is poured into the wood frame. The wood frames are then raised as the building gets taller. In many ways, the conceptual design of a skyscraper is analogous to the human body. The central core is the spine of the building. Without a functioning core, the systems of the building would have no place to reside. Beams and columns are much like the human skeleton in that they give a defining structure to the skyscraper. Finally, the exterior cladding acts like skin and clothing, protecting the building from the elements and keeping its occupants safe.

MECHANICAL SYSTEMS

The central core of a building provides space for ductwork and other utilities that must run to each individual floor. The bulk of the mechanical equipment, however, is generally in one or more centralized locations, such as the top floor of a building or on several floors dedicated to mechanical services.

Service Floors

Many buildings have floors that are only accessible by service elevators, which are large, sturdy elevators used for hauling equipment that is too heavy for a passenger elevator. Generally, there is one service floor for every ten or twelve occupied floors. The mechanical floors and ducts carry many of the "invisible" requirements for making a building habitable; these include heating, air conditioning, and ventilation, which is necessary in skyscrapers with windows that do not open.

It is easy to tell which floors in a skyscraper are used for mechanics and are not occupied. Simply look for the floors that are blacked out and do not contain windows!

Water Storage

Water tanks are located on several floors, partly for sprinkler systems and fire control. Even very large water pumps cannot send water 1,000 feet (300 meters) into the air in the event of a fire, so buildings have water tanks and pumps at least every twelve or fifteen floors. Water used in restrooms and kitchens can also be stored more efficiently throughout a number of floors. Many skyscrapers also have a large water-storage system at or near the top of the building.

To understand why it makes sense to store water in various locations, consider how water is typically dispersed through a large area, such as a town. Most rural areas with a water distribution system have a water tower, which is a tall tower with a water tank on top. The dimensions of these water tanks can range from 15 to 150 feet (3 and 45 meters). The elevated tank supplies additional water pressure for all the houses it supplies with water. The higher the tower, the more water pressure it can provide. For a city, such a tank would hold around one million gallons of water (3.7 million liters), or enough to supply the city for about a day. Water towers can provide large amounts of water at high pressure when needed all at once, such as during the morning shower time, and then slowly refill the tank during the night, when demand is low. This diminishes each home's required pumping capacity.

Modern skyscrapers are taller than the average water tower. Once a building exceeds the average height by such a substantial amount, water towers cannot supply enough pressure for water to reach the top floors. For this reason, most skyscrapers have their own water towers on the roof. Storing water at the top of a tall building raises it to a physically high elevation; this allows the water tank to store the potential energy (energy of position) of the water. Once energy has been exerted to pump the water up to the top of a tall building, the

If a skyscraper is short enough, its water tower might be located on the ground.

Taller buildings can sometimes require that a water tower be constructed on the roof. This provides the gravitational potential energy necessary to increase water pressure within the building.

energy is stored as potential energy until the water is needed. When the rooftop water tank is used, either to meet everyday demands for plumbing from the building's residents or for an emergency, such as a fire, the potential energy is released as kinetic energy. The water flows rapidly down to lower floors, supplying ample water pressure for showers and plenty of volume in case of a fire.

Garbage and Mail

There are several other mechanical considerations for tall buildings, including garbage removal and mail delivery. Most large buildings use garbage chutes made of a high-density material, which lead from maintenance rooms down to central repositories. These save countless hours of manual labor. Skyscraper floors are large, and their occupants generate a considerable amount of waste. It would be impractical for mainte-

GRAVITATIONAL WATER SYSTEMS

The Old Colony Building in Chicago uses a gravitational pressure method for water delivery. It has a large water tank on the top floor but no pumping system. The building uses the original water pipes installed when it was built in 1894, so there is no method for retro-fitting a pump. The owners maintain this rather archaic system because it is still functioning, and replacing it would be a major undertaking.

nance staff to take the elevator every time a portable can was full; garbage chutes allow them to consolidate tasks and work more efficiently. In Australia and other countries, garbage chutes are often installed on the outsides of apartment buildings, perhaps because they were retrofitted rather than included as an initial part of the building's design. In addition to garbage chutes, many large buildings have mail slots that occupants can use to mail letters; these, too, lead to a central repository where postal workers can collect outgoing mail from the entire building.

ELECTRICAL SYSTEMS

Electrical systems within a building provide power for vital elements such as heating, cooling, lighting, and security systems. Heating and cooling is generally global throughout the building with large heaters and air conditioners placed strategically. These systems provide a basic level of climate control for building occupants, who then can fine-tune the temperature of their offices or living spaces by using individual thermostats.

Providing electricity to a skyscraper is conceptually similar to the way a typical house is wired. In a town, power stations with turbine generators use a fuel source, usually fossil fuels, but sometimes nuclear or hydroelectric power, to generate massive amounts of power. Substations and transformers throughout the town lower the voltage that comes into a home's circuit breaker to 220 volts. In very tall skyscrapers, power companies may run high-voltage lines directly into the building to avoid power loss, and then use transformers inside the building to lower the voltage to regular household levels.

In skyscrapers, electrical wiring is generally run through holes in the steel supporting beams. Wires are run above the ceiling to allow power for various uses. Electrical wires are also run down into the walls and along the baseboards to provide electricity to wall sockets for equipment such as computers and copy machines.

Lighting

Modern skyscrapers make use of various types of lights. While most are selected because they efficiently fulfill a specific function, some skyscraper lighting is purely aesthetic. Designers choose certain lights because they highlight parts of the building for a dramatic effect.

Indoor lighting can be divided into several types. Overall lighting does exactly what the term implies. It lights up the building's interior with ceiling fixtures, hallway lights, and other "generic" lights such as those on stairs. Task lighting involves lights installed for specific tasks. Computer desks often have halogen lamps, for example, while a photography darkroom uses a red

Buildings must be visually appealing during both the day and evening; accent lighting helps create a distinct aura for skyscrapers at night.

light. Aesthetic lighting, also called accent lighting, serves to highlight objects that enhance the building's interior, such as artwork. In addition, accent lighting on the building's exterior can show off a skyscraper's setbacks, giving the building an elegant profile when seen at night.

These categories can be further broken down into the type of fixtures. Types of lighting include soffit lighting, which is near the walls, and recessed lighting, which is embedded in the ceiling. Track lighting is also common in office buildings. This consists of lights mounted on a track, which is then attached to the ceiling.

There are many different kinds of interior lighting for tall structures. Rooms, hallways, mechanical spaces, and individual offices all require distinct types of illumination.

The Basics of Light

The first artificial lighting was the incandescent light bulb. The science behind it is straightforward. The light bulb has a threaded metal base with an electrical contact at the bottom. Leading from the base are two metal wires that go into the center of the bulb. These wires hold the filament—a thin strip of tungsten wound into a coil. The glass bulb contains an inert gas, such as argon, and serves to keep oxygen away from the tungsten coil.

When a light bulb is connected to a power source, electric current passes through the filament and heats it to a very high temperature, around 4,000 degrees Fahrenheit (2,200 degrees Celsius). When a material is heated, the energy it absorbs causes electrons bound to the nucleus of each atom to go into an excited state where they move to higher energy levels that are further from the nucleus. An excited atom is unstable, however, and quickly will return to its ground state. As it returns to the ground state, the absorbed energy is given off in the form of a photon, which can be thought of as a particle of light.

Photons have particular energies, depending on how excited the electron was. Higher-energy photons have shorter wavelengths. The wavelength of a photon determines its place on the electromagnetic spectrum. High-energy photons are in the ultraviolet spectrum, with wavelengths too short for the human eye to see. Lower-energy photons are in the infrared spectrum, with wavelengths too long to be seen. This type of radiation is called thermal radiation, or heat. In between the two is the visible spectrum, which spans the colors from red (at a wavelength just shorter than infrared) to violet (at a wavelength just longer than ultraviolet).

When an incandescent light bulb is turned on, the tungsten atoms inside the heated filament absorb electrons, become excited, and give off photons as they return to their unexcited ground state. Much of the light given off by a typical incandescent light bulb with a tungsten filament is in the infrared. Only about 10 percent of the photons from an incandescent light bulb are in the visible range, making this type of lighting fairly inefficient.

Office buildings, as well as schools and even some homes, often make use of fluorescent rather than incandescent lights, because they are much

The electromagnetic spectrum is made up of electromagnetic radiation at various wavelengths. Short-wavelength, high-energy radiations such as x-rays are at one end, and long-wavelength, lower-energy radio waves are at the other. Visible light is located in the middle, and each color has a different wavelength.

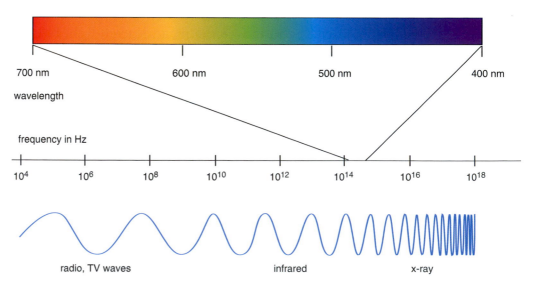

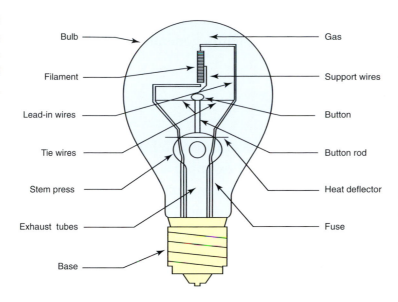

Incandescent light bulbs involve a filament, gas and support wires.

Bulb
Filament
Lead-in wires
Tie wires
Stem press
Exhaust tubes
Base

Gas
Support wires
Button
Button rod
Heat deflector
Fuse

more energy efficient. Fluorescent lamps use a sealed tube that contains a gas, such as argon, plus liquid mercury. The inside of the glass tube is coated with a powdered material called phosphor, which is made up of chemical compounds that give off light when light falls on them, hence the term phosphorescent. There are electrodes at either end of the tube, and once the fluorescent light is turned on, the voltage causes electrons to move between the tube's ends. Some of the liquid mercury vaporizes and interacts with the moving electrons. When electrons collide with the mercury atoms, they cause the mercury to give off high-energy photons. These photons then bounce off the tube's phosphor coating, resulting in visible light that is transmitted through the glass.

The color of fluorescent light can be varied by changing the chemical composition of the phosphor coating on the inside of the tube. Fluorescent lights are efficient and capable of lighting large areas because of the long

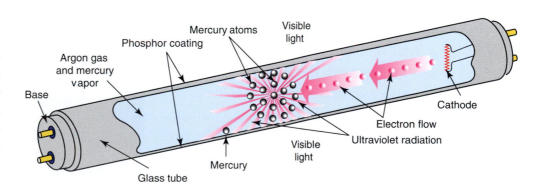

Fluorescent light bulbs can emit a very bright glow, without heating up enough to burn your fingers.

Mercury atoms
Visible light
Phosphor coating
Argon gas and mercury vapor
Base
Cathode
Electron flow
Ultraviolet radiation
Visible light
Mercury
Glass tube

tubes, but may flicker in very cold temperatures because the lamp cannot create enough heat to consistently generate light photons.

ELECTRICAL FIRES

Has poor electrical wiring ever caused a building disaster? Unfortunately, the answer is yes. One recent example is the Windsor Tower Building in Madrid, which caught fire due to a circuit-breaker failure in February 2005. The building was well designed, with two concrete floors intended to provide extra strength. There was some amount of fireproofing on the steel frame and the designers specified concrete columns around the perimeter of the structure. Fortunately, these design elements helped to prevent the building's collapse. The interior of the building, however, was completely burned out from the flames.

SAFETY FEATURES

In addition to the necessary functional building systems, other features are required for a skyscraper to be a safe place to inhabit. Like any other habitable building, skyscrapers must have smoke detectors and fire escape systems so that, in the event of a fire, people can evacuate the building quickly and safely.

Smoke alarms work on the simple premise that loud noise will alert people to fire. While there are several types of smoke detectors, the most common ones use an ionization chamber to detect smoke. This chamber contains a radioactive material, which generates alpha particles. These particles ionize the air inside the chamber, creating a current. In the

Spain's Windsor Tower was built in 1979, but succumbed to fire in 2005.

event of a fire, smoke entering the detector interrupts the current. This drop in current triggers an electronic cylinder to emit an annoying loud noise, thereby alerting the building occupants to the smoke.

When fire breaks out in a skyscraper and the alarms do their job, people inside the building are directed to the nearest possible exit. Elevators are not used during a fire because they will likely fail to work properly due to the smoke. Stairways are the best way for skyscraper occupants to exit the building, despite the fact that people on the upper floors may have a great number of stairs to walk down! All skyscrapers are equipped with multiple sets of stairways; the exact number will depend on the size of the building and the floor layout. Stairs are housed inside stairwells, which are constructed of concrete or another material with inherent fireproofing.

Can the steel itself melt in a fire? While the exact melting point of steel depends on the precise alloy used, steel beams and columns will fail if a fire reaches a high enough temperature for a sustained period. Iron, for example, has a melting point of 2,795 degrees Fahrenheit (1,535 degrees Celsius). While gasoline burns at around 1,500 degrees Fahrenheit (950 degrees Celsius), jet fuel burns at nearly twice that temperature.

To protect steel in the event of a skyscraper fire, structural steel elements are coated in fireproofing. Exposed steel members are usually painted using an intumescent paint, or one that swells up when exposed to heat. The paint thickens greatly, giving the fire extra material to burn through, and thereby protecting the steel for a longer period. Structural steel that is hidden behind walls is usually sprayed with a fireproof coating typically made of gypsum, another substance that slows the pace at which a fire will reach the steel. Slowing the fire allows the steel to stand for a longer period of time, which in turn gives the building occupants more time to evacuate to safety.

Skyscraper design is quite a complex endeavor. Building structure must be considered in combination with cladding. Mechanical and other functional systems are also required elements, as are various safety features designed to help protect the lives of the building's inhabitants. One of the most important overall considerations, though, is the combination of loads that the skyscraper must bear. Wind, snow, and even gravity are forces that structural engineers will take into account, and the design response to these forces helps shape the overall skyscraper.

THE WOOLWORTH BUILDING

One of New York's oldest skyscrapers, the Woolworth Building was the world's tallest building for seventeen years—between 1913 and 1930. Commissioned by retailer Frank Winfield Woolworth and designed by architect Cass Gilbert, the building still stands in a prominent Manhattan location at the corner of Park Place and Broadway.

The Woolworth chain of "five-and-dime" stores began with Frank Woolworth's first store in 1878. By the time the Woolworth Building was completed in 1913, Woolworth's was the preeminent retailer of a variety of low-cost goods. The chain introduced a number of important innovations in retail. Products were displayed for customers to examine directly, which was a change from earlier stores in which all goods were kept behind the shopkeeper's counter. Some stores had lunch counters, which allowed customers to relax and extend their shopping. As competition emerged in the 1980s, though, the Woolworth chain became less and less popular and closed for good in the 1990s.

The Woolworth Building measures 792 feet (241 meters) in height. Ironically, this is about half the height of the world's tallest building today. It is divided into a massive three-story base level, followed by fifty-two floors of office space clad with terra-cotta panels. The top floors have a decorated pinnacle sitting on top, giving the building its distinctive appearance.

This skyscraper was built in an architectural style known as neo-Gothic, meaning it has elements reminiscent of Gothic architecture. The Gothic period, prevalent in Europe between the twelfth and fifteenth centuries C.E., was characterized by very elaborate cathedrals with features such as high vaulted ceilings, pointed arches, and intricate decorations that included gargoyles. The Woolworth Building incorporates many of these elements into its design. Soon after construction, the building was nicknamed the "Cathedral of Commerce," partly for its impressive height, and partly because its decorative architecture resembled that of a Gothic cathedral.

Structurally, the Woolworth Building is a steel-framed skyscraper clad in masonry. The masonry facade and interior gave Gilbert the perfect opportunity to recreate Gothic elements. On the exterior, Gilbert used terra-cotta panels and piers to mimic a Gothic cathedral. The building's lobby features mosaics, vaulted ceilings, and Gothic-style sculpture—there are even gargoyle statues in the lobby. Showing off his sense of humor, owner and department store magnate Frank Woolworth had caricatures of himself and the architect sculpted and placed in the lobby.

The Woolworth Building in New York, designed by Cass Gilbert and constructed in 1913, is one of the city's oldest surviving skyscrapers and has elaborate terra-cotta decoration on the exterior.

FORCES OF NATURE

If skyscrapers existed in a vacuum, a completely empty space free of outside forces such as wind and other atmospheric effects, their design and structure would be much simpler than they need to be in the real world. But skyscrapers must be designed to withstand the forces of nature, such as gravity, wind, and earthquakes. These real-world forces are some of the strongest that a building must tolerate. Ranging from everyday factors like gravity to once-in-a-lifetime events like an earthquake, these forces affect every aspect of the design process.

GRAVITY

Skyscrapers in proximity to one another can create their own mini-atmosphere, complete with microclimates.

Gravity is the force that attracts objects toward the center of the Earth. From a child's tower of blocks to a soaring skyscraper, all buildings have a natural tendency to fall to the ground. Because the inclination of a building's upper floors would be to fall through its lower floors, the structure of a building must counteract that gravitational force. The heavy construction materials used in a skyscraper must therefore be structurally arranged so as to prevent such a collapse, and the lower levels must be strong enough to support the upper ones.

For this reason, many early brick skyscrapers were built with heavy, wide bases and then became thinner and elongated as they reached higher elevations. The invention of iron and steel allowed designers to use long, thin beams with a very high load-carrying capacity, which led to skyscraper designs that were taller and thinner than the earlier masonry structures. The use of reinforced concrete allowed for stronger, fireproof structures that could climb higher still, partially due to the nature of the reinforcing steel bars inside the concrete. With the additional tensile strength of the steel, these walls could be built thinner and higher, thereby eliminating the chunky appearance of their predecessors.

WIND

Wind is another major force that acts on tall buildings. Unlike gravity, which pulls things downward, wind is usually a horizontal force. Depending on its strength, the wind can push the top of a building as much as a few feet or even a couple of meters, which is definitely enough to make the occupants suffer from motion sickness. A skyscraper's frame must allow enough sway to prevent cracking in the facade or structure, but it must also minimize this movement so that occupants can tolerate being inside the building on a windy day. Another danger created by wind is that the swaying of a building can approach a resonance, where the period of forcing matches the natural period of oscillation of a built structure. One way to understand resonance is to think of a child being pushed on a swing by a parent. As the child swings back and forth, the parent pushes the swing. If the pushes occur at random points in the swing's trajectory, the motion will not build up and the swing will not go very fast or very high. However, if the parent times the pushes so that they always occur at a particular point in the swing's trajectory, namely, when the swing is at its highest point, the period of the pushes matches the period of the swing, and the motion is amplified. This causes the swing to go higher and higher.

In the case of a building, if the time interval between wind gusts happens to line up with the natural period at which the building is swaying, resonance can occur. Resonance can cause the amplitude of the building's motion to increase dramatically and can result in structural failure if it goes unchecked. Engineers employ a number of different techniques to reduce sway.

Structural Supports

One method of minimizing sway that was developed and refined in the first half of the twentieth century was to strengthen the building's central core. A stiff center provides additional bracing when it is attached to the steel structural skeleton, thereby making the entire building less susceptible to excessive wind sway.

For relatively short buildings of about twenty-five stories or less, sway can largely be dealt with in the structure's design. A structural grid consisting of columns and girders is usually sufficient to keep lateral forces in check. Once a building reaches a certain height, though, additional bracing is usually required. Shear walls, specifically designed to resist lateral forces such as wind and earthquakes, provide this extra support. In typical house construction, for example, a wood-frame stud wall alone is not a shear wall. But when lateral cross bracing is added in the form of plywood or other panels, it becomes a shear wall. In a large skyscraper, shear walls are typically made of reinforced concrete.

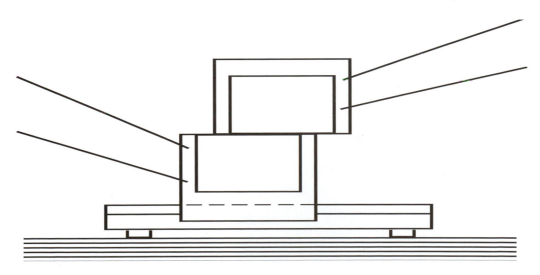

Shear force is present when two objects slide past one another.

The John Hancock Center in Chicago was constructed in 1969, rises to 100 stories, and contains fifty elevators. The X-bracing on the outside demonstrates the building's tubular structural system.

Hollow Tubes

To achieve wind resistance, some skyscrapers use a design methodology known as hollow-tube construction. The 100-story John Hancock Center in Chicago uses this approach. Built in 1969 and designed by the architectural firm of Skidmore, Owings, and Merrill, the building is surrounded by a dense array of steel columns around its exterior edge. These are tied together with massive diagonal braces visible on the outside of the building; together these features form a stiff structure capable of resisting hefty lateral loads. Conceptually, the building can be seen as one enormous vertical truss or integrated structural frame. It is one of the few skyscrapers to have such clear structural expression.

In this case, the X-braces and the exterior columns together make up the steel tube. Aesthetically, this building is unusual because the structure is completely revealed on the outside rather than being hidden in the interior. It shows how the building is able to stand so tall. The exterior facade, made of anodized aluminum and tinted glass, contributes to the building's overall sleekness.

The Sears Tower, also in Chicago, makes use of a different type of tube design—a series of bundled tubes. This 110-story skyscraper, also designed by Skidmore, Owings, and Merrill, was completed in 1973. Sears, Roebuck, and Company was the nation's largest retailer in the late 1960s, so it was only natural that it would want the world's tallest building as its icon. The Sears Tower was the tallest building in the world until 1996 and is still the tallest building in the United States.

As with a more conventional tube skyscraper, a rigid network of beams and columns along the exterior supports the Sears Tower. These rigid walls together form a tube. For aesthetic reasons, as well as to maximize floor space as the building rose in height, the designers packed nine of these tubes side by side. Each tube is 75 feet (22 meters) wide with a clear-span interior, meaning there are no interior structural elements breaking up the space. The tubes' heights are not the same. Two are 108 floors tall, three are 90 floors tall, two are 66 floors tall, and two are 50 floors tall. The staggered heights of the tubes increase the building's overall wind resistance, because there is a smaller cross-section to catch wind forces at its uppermost heights.

Mass Dampers

In addition to structural tubes, another method of dealing with wind sway is with a tuned mass damper. This heavy concrete block, positioned on one of the upper floors of a sky-scraper, can weigh more than 400 tons (363 metric tons). It moves by oil, springs, or some other mechanism that pushes the weight from side to side to counteract the wind or other forces acting upon the building. As the building begins to move to the left, for example, the tuned mass moves to the right, a process that effectively damps the overall movement of the building.

Another one of Chicago's best-known skyscrapers, the Sears Tower was the world's tallest building until it was surpassed by Taipei 101.

The block moves in the opposite direction of the force because the block is tuned to have the same natural frequency as that of the building. Since the mass and the building move at the same frequency, when the inertia of the mass is overcome by the external force, the springs holding the mass in position push it at the same pace as the building itself, but in the opposite direction.

Super-tall buildings often use tuned mass dampers to help reduce the effects of wind sway. This huge, 730-ton (662 metric ton) damper is located in the Taipei 101 building.

Tuned mass dampers are used in many skyscrapers. One of the first was New York's Citicorp Center. This 1977 skyscraper, designed by architect Hugh Stubbins, rises to a height of 915 feet (279 meters). A 400-ton (363-metric ton) concrete mass was installed on one of the top floors. It sat in a bed of oil, which allowed it to slide back and forth.

The Physics of Mass Dampers

The basic physics concepts at work in a mass damper are those of momentum and inertia. Newton's first law of motion states that any object, once in motion, will stay in motion unless acted on by some external force. Similarly, if an object is at rest, it will stay at rest unless acted upon by some force. This concept is called inertia. Momentum (P) is a quantity possessed by any object in motion and is described as the product of the object's mass (m) and velocity (v):

$$P = m \times v$$

A tuned mass damper remains at rest until acted upon by a force, such as the wind force acting on a building. The force of the wind causes the mass of the building to move at a particular velocity, giving the building momentum. The tuned mass damper, however, is not statically connected to the rest of the building, and its inertia can help offset the momentum of the building. Instead of all the force of the wind going into moving the building, some of that force is transferred into trying to move the mass damper and overcome its inertia. The damper is constructed so that it is subject to friction, such as by requiring a mass to move through a thick fluid like oil.

In this way, instead of all the transferred force going into moving the mass damper, a substantial portion of it is dissipated as friction. Friction is the force of resistance that results when two objects move against each other. Friction (Fr) is calculated as a product of the normal (perpendicular) force (N) and what is called the coefficient of friction (μ):

$$Fr = \mu N$$

The normal force is the force that pushes two objects together. Suppose a child pushes a toy car along a table. The normal force is the amount of force the child exerts on the car in order to make it move. The coefficient of friction is a value based on the roughness of the two surfaces that are coming into contact, such as the wheels of the toy car and the surface of the table. This value has a range between zero and infinity. When calculating friction forces, the correct value for the coefficient of friction is most easily obtained by looking it up in a physics table, though the values may change depending on how clean or wet the surfaces are.

The oil surrounding a typical tuned mass damper allows the mass to be decoupled from the rest of the building, reducing the coefficient of friction and allowing the mass to move freely. A thick, viscous fluid such as oil also provides friction as the mass moves. Friction results in a transfer of kinetic energy into heat energy and is said to dissipate heat from the system. The net result of a tuned mass damper system is that it transforms

When two rough surfaces rub against each other, significant frictional heating can be generated. This friction can result in sparks because of the high amount of heat contained in the tiny metal fragments that fly out when metal collides with metal.

the force applied by the wind. Instead of allowing all of the wind force to go into moving the top floors of a skyscraper back and forth, the damper results in a substantial portion of that force being dissipated harmlessly as heat that radiates from the system. Frictional heating is fairly inefficient, so large amounts of kinetic energy can be dissipated without fear of overheating.

Mass dampers are convenient because the system is a closed one that is self-contained and does not require anything outside of itself to function. As soon as the wind stops blowing, the motion of the building and the mass damper slow down and eventually return to their rest positions. The system does not require any intervention or resetting to make it ready for the next gust of wind.

Welds and Wind

A building's ability to withstand the wind can also involve structural considerations. In the case of the Citicorp Center in New York, a serious engineering challenge resulted from a lack of attention

New York's Citicorp Center (constructed in 1977) has a distinctly angled top, which stands out in the Manhattan skyline.

to wind force. When construction on the skyscraper was completed in 1978, the primary engineer, William LeMessurier, realized, with the help of a student, that the bolted connections throughout the structure were not strong enough for the maximum predicted

WELDING VERSUS SOLDERING

How is welding different from soldering? In welding, two pieces of metal are completely fused; filler is used to add to the strength of the joint, but does not come between the two pieces of metal. Soldered joints use a solder, which is an alloy with a low melting point, to connect two pieces of material. With soldering, the solder itself forms the bond. With welding, the metals bond directly to each other.

wind speed at the site, which was in excess of 70 miles per hour (113 kilometers per hour). The problem arose because of a late change from welded to bolted connections. Welding is a process in which two pieces of metal are permanently connected using heat. Some type of filler material is added into the resulting joint so that, once fused, a visible connection is seen.

There is little possibility of failure in a welded connection aside from cracking of the material itself, so welded joints generally stand up very well to wind and other loads. Bolted joints, on the other hand, have a higher potential for failure because the bolts can break or come loose. The engineer was able to rectify the problem by having plates welded over the most critical bolted connections in the Citicorp Center, thereby avoiding a potential crisis.

EARTHQUAKES

Tuned mass dampers are also very useful in case of earthquakes, another source of lateral force. Earthquakes result from the movement of earth around underground faults or volcanic activity and can have catastrophic results.

A recent example of tuned mass damping is the Taipei Financial Center, commonly known as Taipei 101, which is currently the tallest building in the world. Located in Taipei, Taiwan, the building, completed in 2004, reaches a height of 1,671 feet (509 meters). Because of its extreme height, the building required extra measures to minimize the amount of wind sway experienced by its occupants and to provide extra reinforcement in the event of an earthquake.

Typhoons are another force of nature that building designers must consider in Taiwan. These tropical storms, which originate in the North Pacific or China Sea, can bring winds of up to 74 miles per hour (120 kilometers per hour), so their impact on tall buildings is considerable. To compensate for the predicted forces from wind and earthquakes, a 730-ton (662-metric ton) tuned mass damper was installed on the eighty-eighth floor of Taipei 101. When engaged, the mass is capable of damping approximately 35 percent of the building's sway.

Skyscrapers, especially those located near known fault zones, must be designed to withstand the occasional force of an earthquake. Tuned mass dampers are an effective way to deal with these forces, as is additional lateral bracing of the structural frame. Foundations are also dug deeper than

Taipei 101 set many records for height and design, and has been lauded by Newsweek magazine as one of the Seven New Wonders of the World.

WIND ENERGY

Wind is a substantial force, one that can be harnessed into energy. How is wind converted into electric power? Windmills or wind turbines, which are essentially large, stable pinwheels, are placed in high-wind areas. As the blades of the windmill turn, they turn the shaft that connects blades to a generator. The rotation force is converted into electrical power using magnetic fields. Power is then delivered to a transformer and distributed to the local power grid.

usual for skyscrapers in earthquake territory, as this helps ensure that the building is firmly anchored to the ground.

ZONING LEGISLATION

Architects and engineers do not have free rein in the design of any building, and skyscrapers are no exception. Once super-tall buildings began appearing, legislation was enacted to control their growth and development. The most notable piece of legislation was the New York City Building Zone Resolution of 1916, which regulated the height of skyscrapers and instituted some of the first so-called setback laws.

A setback is a recession, or a spot in a building's facade where there is a break in the vertical face. Part of the building behind the front facade may go on to increase in height, creating a stair-step pattern in the building's profile. One of the main reasons for requiring setbacks was that very tall buildings cast very long shadows on neighboring buildings, making the city streets darker than they had been. Setbacks cause a building's cross-

Legislation was enacted to force skyscrapers to step back as they rose in height, mainly so that they would cast shorter shadows onto neighboring buildings and streets.

section to become progressively smaller, resulting in less intrusive shadows. Chicago and other cities followed New York's lead in passing setback legislation over the years.

The heart of a skyscraper's engineering design lies in the building's response to loads. These loads change dramatically depending on many factors, including the building's physical location. Earthquake loads, for example, are nonexistent in parts of the world that are not susceptible to earthquakes. Disaster can strike in many forms, and skyscrapers have had their fair share. Read on to learn about some of history's more infamous skyscraper debacles.

SKYSCRAPER DEMOLITIONS AND DISASTERS

Skyscrapers "grew up," literally, around the Brooklyn Bridge.

The history of skyscraper development, while mainly a story of success and innovation, is also sprinkled with the occasional tale of demolition or destruction. In the early years, high rises were built to serve a certain need, only to be demolished some years later. Why go to the trouble and expense of building a skyscraper, only to tear it down? This practice is not a common one today; but years ago, as new building techniques evolved and the need for more office and living space increased, skyscrapers were torn down to make room for larger buildings, or to make room for another construction project. There have also been a few true skyscraper disasters. These events, while horrendous, hold lessons about the physics of skyscrapers under extreme stress.

PULITZER BUILDING (1890–1955) AND TRIBUNE BUILDING (1875–1955)

The construction of the Brooklyn Bridge in the second half of the nineteenth century was an enormous effort that employed thousands of New York's construction workers. The bridge also occupied a substantial portion of the city. When the Brooklyn Bridge was expanded in 1955 due to construction for the new automobile entrance, two major skyscrapers stood in the way of the plans: the Pulitzer Building and the Tribune Building. The Pulitzer Building, also known as the World Building after publisher Joseph Pulitzer's *New York World*, was a tower designed by George B. Post that stood 309 feet (94 meters) high. This skyscraper was the tallest in New York City for a time, surpassing Trinity Church when it was built in 1890. As Trinity Church was a dominant element of the Manhattan skyline at this time, passing it was a considerable feat.

The New York Tribune Building and the Pulitzer Building (also called the World Building) helped shape the New York skyline in the late nineteenth century.

One unusual fact about the Pulitzer Building is that while it was constructed using a steel frame, the exterior cladding was also structural. The masonry walls were designed to help support part of the structure, rather than being hung off the steel frame (as was the case in later skyscrapers). The building represented an important transitional milestone in the development of the steel-frame high rise.

The New York Tribune Building, designed by Richard Morris Hunt in 1875, was a truly gorgeous building, combining different-colored brick and bearing a signature clock tower. The building debuted at nine stories, but nine additional stories were added in 1905. It was home to the offices of the *New York Tribune*, a major newspaper started in 1841 by Horace Greeley.

Together, the two buildings created a news hub in Manhattan. Sadly, these two pieces of New York history were demolished, and exist today only in photographs, sketches, and written documentation.

MANHATTAN LIFE INSURANCE COMPANY BUILDING (1894–1930)

Another sad story of skyscraper demise is that of the Manhattan Life Insurance Company building. Completed in 1894, it was the tallest building in the world at the time of construction and was clad primarily in granite and brick. Its design was the result of a competition held by Manhattan Life Insurance Company.

The first skyscraper to reach more than 100 feet (30 meters) in height, the Manhattan Life Insurance building was a major presence in New York between 1894 and 1930.

By 1930, it was no longer the tallest or most interesting building in the world, and advocates of historic preservation lost the battle to maintain this regal structure. It was demolished in 1930 and replaced by the corporate headquarters for the Irving Trust Company, which became One Wall Street.

MASONIC TEMPLE (1892–1939)

New York and Chicago were the forerunners in the skyscraper race, and both destroyed some of their oldest buildings in the early twentieth century. The Masonic Temple in Chicago, completed in 1892, was designed by famed architect Daniel Burnham, who created the world's tallest building at the time with this 302-foot (92-meter) project. It was surpassed in height by the Manhattan Life Insurance Company building two years later.

Like most tall buildings at the time, it used a steel structural frame with brick and stone facades. Its gabled top story, unusual for a skyscraper, gave the building a more intimate, house-like feeling. Despite winning awards and other acclaim, it was deemed too old-fashioned in 1939 and was demolished.

Chicago's Masonic Temple was built in 1892 and was the world's tallest building at the time, but was demolished in 1939.

JOHN HANCOCK TOWER OF BOSTON

Not all stories of troubled skyscrapers end in their ultimate demise. One example of a skyscraper that overcame technical difficulties is the John Hancock Tower in Boston. Designed by well-known architect I.M. Pei and the firm of Pei, Cobb, and Freed, and opened in 1976, it is by far the tallest building in the area and is a clearly visible landmark throughout the city. It rises to its full 790-foot (240-meter) height in mirrored elegance, with more than 10,000 blue-tinted windows covering its steel frame, most of which reflect the city around them.

These windows, however, were a major headache for the building's designers. Soon after the building was completed, the windows began to fall out. Whenever the wind blew hard enough, massive windows, some weighing as much as 500 pounds (225 kilograms), detached from the steel frame and went sailing down to the sidewalk below. While lawsuits prevented the true cause from being fully disclosed, most speculation focused on unanticipated wind pressure against the outside of the building. Another possible explanation is in the heat differential between outside and inside. If the windows were not set with proper expansion joints, excess heat on either side of the pane could cause it to swell and pop out. Similarly, excess cold on one side would cause shrinkage, which also resulted in the loss of the windows.

The building was supposed to open to the public in 1971, but these problems delayed the

The John Hancock Tower in Boston is infamous for raining glass panels down onto the sidewalk below.

Partly because it was missing panes of glass, the Hancock Tower required extensive repair before the building could be safely occupied

opening. The windows were replaced with heat-treated glass and special sensors were put into each one so that the building managers would know ahead of time if panes were about to fall out. The problem was resolved at that point, and the building became safe for occupation.

Another problem with the Hancock Tower came into play even before construction began. When the foundations were dug, steel retaining walls (instead of a more conventional concrete slurry wall) were put into the pit to keep earth from filling it back up. Unfortunately, these walls soon warped. This massive pressure caused a chain reaction, cracking both pavement in neighboring sidewalks and foundation structures in nearby buildings.

ONE NEW YORK PLAZA

On August 5, 1970, fire ripped through the thirty-third story of the fifty-story One New York Plaza, eventually spreading to two floors. In a tragic twist, two people died when the elevator car they were in stopped at the thirty-third floor and would not close its doors. Investigations later determined that the fireproof coating that was supposed to be protecting the steel beams of the building had broken off in many places. The beams were left unprotected and started to collapse in the high heat, and the damage and death toll could have been much higher if the fire had taken longer to contain and if the concrete floor slabs had also given way.

As a result of this tragic event, new codes were put in place stating that, for all public buildings, any beams or floors damaged by fire must be replaced, not just repaired. This significant change ensured much safer buildings with less risk of their succumbing to fire, since the fireproofing would be intact.

Another change was related to elevator safety. Most elevators use a beam of light to determine if a person or object is blocking the door. This is why elevator doors do not shut while people are passing through them. In this case, the smoke from the fire blocked the beam, so the doors stayed open. Because of this disaster, a new code was created to ensure that, in the event of a fire, elevators would be taken out of service unless specifically overridden by a firefighter.

In addition, before this fire, designers and engineers had developed the concept of a fire-resistant building as one in which a fire could not spread beyond its originating floor. One New York Plaza was believed to be fire resistant, but after the fire, in which two stories were affected, it was clear that this concept itself was flawed. From this point forward, no buildings were considered fire resistant, and fire safety precautions had to include the whole building.

FIRST INTERSTATE BANK BUILDING

Another historic skyscraper fire occurred at the First Interstate Bank Building in Los Angeles. In May 1988, a fire broke out late at night in this sixty-two–story skyscraper. The building was a typical 1980s skyscraper, with a steel frame, and glass and aluminum cladding. By the time the fire was put out more than three hours after it began, one person was dead and thirty-five were injured, and nearly five floors had been ravaged by flames, smoke, and water damage.

The worst skyscraper fire in Los Angeles history, this disaster called on more than fifty fire companies to try to save the building. Remarkably, there was no major damage to the steel frame, most likely because of the thick fireproof coating that was much more durable than that used in the One New York Plaza building. Secondary and floor beams had to be replaced, as did many broken windows, but the skyscraper itself remained structurally sound.

While the battle to put the fire out was a success overall, there were a few hiccups. While more than 90 percent of the building was equipped with sprinklers, some of the valves were closed at the time and were ineffective. The firefighters' water helped douse the flames, but also rendered most of the building's electrical and telephone systems unusable. Also, emergency radios did not work throughout much of the building because of interference from the structural steel skeleton.

This 1988 fire at Los Angeles' First Interstate Bank was one of the worst that city had known.

FIREPROOFING

One explanation for the minor fire damage to the First Interstate Bank Building is fireproofing. The structural steel beams were coated with a fire-resistant material that helped delay damage until the fire could be put out. Today, fireproofing solution is sprayed onto many steel structures, and each spray has a rating. A one-hour rating, for example, means the substance would give firefighters an hour before the beam begins to lose structural integrity. A two-hour rating would last two hours, and so on. These spray-on coatings tend to be puffy and unsuitable for indoor use, however; so intumescent paint is often used for coating interior beams. Intumescent paints are flame retardant and physically expand when exposed to fire. This expansion protects the structure beneath and gives firefighters more time to do their job.

WORLD TRADE CENTER TOWERS (1973–2001)

Before the events of September 11, 2001, the twin towers at the World Trade Center were jewels in the New York City skyline. These 110-story towers made a considerable impression when construction was completed in 1973, and they brought with them several interesting building innovations. They used a steel tube design and had a major exterior structural system paired with a supporting interior core. Because the buildings were so tall, wind sway was a major issue for both the stability of the towers and the motion sickness of their occupants. More than 10,000 dampers were incorporated into various structural elements to reduce the effects of heavy winds on the overall building.

But the technological brilliance that went into the construction of the towers could not save them from the terrorist attack of September 11, 2001. Boeing commercial airliners were flown into each of the two towers

September 11, 2001, is a date that is permanently engraved in the minds of New Yorkers who witnessed the falling of the World Trade Center.

by hijackers. While the towers withstood the initial impacts admirably, hours later each tower fell to the ground. The main reason behind their ultimate collapse was the fires that burned inside each tower. Steel has a very high melting point. It begins to lose strength at 1,200 degrees Fahrenheit (650 degrees Celsius) and melts at 2,750 degrees Fahrenheit (1,510 degrees Celsius). Burning jet fuel took its toll on the steel structure, causing many weaknesses and eventually the towers' collapse.

THE EMPIRE STATE BUILDING PLANE CRASH

Perhaps surprisingly, the World Trade Center towers were not the first skyscrapers to be hit by an airplane. New York's Empire State Building, completed in 1931, was the world's tallest skyscraper until 1972. The building was designed in the Art Deco style and was one of the first sky-scrapers to use setbacks.

The Empire State Building had a run-in with an airplane in 1945. Lieutenant Colonel William Smith flew a military B-25 bomber over New York City on July 28. It was an extremely foggy day, and Smith flew

The Empire State Building was the unlucky recipient of an accidental plane crash in 1945.

lower than usual, hoping to drop below the fog line. Regulations at the time dictated that planes fly no lower than 2,000 feet (600 meters), but Smith was hovering only a bit over 900 feet (275 meters) from the ground. When he veered his plane off course quickly to avoid hitting the New York Central Building, he flew into the seventy-ninth floor of the Empire State Building's north face. Even though it was a Saturday, there were people working in the building, and fourteen people (eleven occupants and the three-man bomber crew) were killed that day from the flames that erupted from the burning jet fuel.

The setbacks of the building played a key role in preventing falling debris from hurting people on the sidewalks below. While one engine and other parts of the plane did fall to the ground, most of the debris landed on top of the setbacks many floors up. Because the damage was localized and the fires quickly contained, the stability of the overall building remained intact.

Though it quickly became known that the building had been hit by an airplane and not intentionally bombed, the fears racing through people's minds were probably much like those of New Yorkers after the 2001 attack on the World Trade Center. World War II was winding down and, for those inside the Empire State Building at the time of the crash, it felt like they were under attack. Fortunately, the incident was both isolated and accidental.

Disasters come in many forms. Whether due to natural causes, terrorist attack, or sheer accident, skyscrapers suffer the consequences of these events, and, because of their very large size, the effects are often more exaggerated than with smaller buildings. However, careful design—and good fortune—helps ensure that skyscrapers remain as safe as possible for their occupants. Skyscraper designers are responsible for all aspects of the building's structure and function, and safety is always a foremost concern.

GLOSSARY

Aesthetic—of concern in the visual realm; a way to define beauty

Aesthetic lighting—a lighting design for a building's interior or exterior that is not purely functional, but rather serves to highlight objects; accent lighting

Alloy—a combination of at least two elements, at least one of which is metal

Art Deco—a movement in art and architecture that took place between 1925 and 1940; design typical of this period used chrome and other metals, in addition to sharp geometric forms

Bessemer converter—a special furnace that creates steel from pig iron; part of the equipment involved in the Bessemer process

Bessemer process—a method for making cast iron more flexible by removing carbon and impurities from it

Cast iron—an iron alloy that contains between 1.8 and 4.5 percent carbon

Chicago School—an architectural style emerging in the late 1800s/early 1900s

Cladding—materials that are used to cover or seal a building's exterior

Counterweight—a large mass that counterbalances the weight of an object in motion, such as an elevator car loaded with people

Cross-section—the two-dimensional shape created by a slice through the center of an object; for example, the cross-section of a cylinder is a circle if sliced from side to side, or a rectangle if sliced from end to end

Curtain wall—non–load-bearing exterior wall of a building that supports only its own weight; is hung from the building's steel frame using metal hangers

Damper—in skyscrapers, a movable device that is used to modulate the oscillation of a building under extreme conditions, such as high winds or earthquake

Dead load—the permanent weight of the materials used to make a building

Decouple—to sever or disconnect

Dissipate—to disperse or break up and go in separate directions

Earthquake—a trembling, or shaking, of the Earth's crust, caused by motion within the Earth along a fault line or due to volcanic activity

Expansion joint—a break in a construction joint that allows for building materials to expand and contract

Facade—exterior surface or walls of a building

Fireproofing—material applied to portions of a building that increases its resistance to fire

Float glass—a type of glass created when molten glass is floated in a pressurized tin bath and made into perfectly flat panes

Fluorescent lamp—a type of lamp that produces light via a phosphor coating that transforms ultraviolet radiation into visible light

Fossil fuel—naturally occurring fuel, such as natural gas, oil, or coal

Foundation—lowest structural support for a building

Friction—force of resistance that is seen when two objects move against each other

Gravity—attractive force between objects; the force that pulls objects toward Earth

Green building—a method of construction that minimizes the impact of the building on both the landscape and our natural resources

High rise—any building taller than 115 feet (35 meters)

Hydraulic—a mechanical system that in some way relies on a liquid, usually oil or water, for motion

Incandescent—glowing with heat

Incompressible fluid—a fluid that retains a constant density regardless of changes in pressure at a constant temperature

Inertia—a property of any material in motion that allows it to stay in motion unless acted on by some external force; a property by which matter remains at rest if not acted upon

Ingot—metal that has been cast into a particular shape

International Style—a period of architectural design that was popular between the 1930s and 1970s; characteristics of this period include open floor plans, glass and steel structural elements, and minimally decorated exteriors

Intumescent paint—a type of flame-retardant paint used in building construction

Kinetic energy—the energy of a body in motion

Landfill—an outdoor area used for waste disposal; if created from excess rock and earth, it can be covered in soil to create new, habitable land

Limestone—a type of sedimentary rock made of calcium carbonate; used for early skyscraper cladding and other building applications

Liquid—a fluid with a fixed volume; not a solid or gas

Load-bearing masonry—a stone building method in which the walls support the weight of the building

Masonry—the portions of a building or other structure that are made out of materials that can be tiled together from separate pieces to create one coherent surface; usually made of brick, stone, tile, or concrete

Modulation—a change, as in that from a higher to lower frequency

Momentum—a quality of any object in motion; the product of the object's mass and velocity

Mullion—thin vertical and horizontal bars that divide windows

Neo-Gothic—an architectural style with elements reminiscent of Gothic architecture

Orthogonal—placed at right angles

Overall lighting—a lighting design for a building's interior that generally includes ceiling fixtures, hallway lights, and other "generic" lights

Passivity—property relating to metal that is coated in an oxide layer

Phosphor—a material that glows when it is exposed to light or to electrons

Piston—a cylindrical piece of equipment, usually hollow, that works with cylinders to form the components of an engine

Pulley—a wheel with grooves along the edge; used with other pulleys to transfer or reverse a force

Rebar—abbreviated term for reinforcing steel bars often used in reinforced concrete

Recessed lighting—lighting embedded into a wall or ceiling

Reinforced concrete—the material resulting when concrete is poured and hardened over steel reinforcing bars

Resistance—in electricity, opposition to the flow of current

Resonance—the particular natural frequency of any object or system at which the object will oscillate at maximum amplitude

Retaining wall—a wall that is constructed to hold back soil

Seismic load—the force caused by earthquakes or other seismic activity

Setback—a recession, or a spot in a building's facade where there is a break; used extensively during the Art Deco period in skyscraper construction to give the buildings a smaller footprint at higher elevations

Shear wall—a braced wall designed specifically to resist lateral forces such as wind and earthquakes

Silica sand—a type of sand with a higher than usual concentration of silicon dioxide

Skyscraper—originally a nautical term that referred to a moon sail, or a triangular sail used on certain types of sailing ships such as the clipper ship; today refers to a class of very tall buildings

Slip forming—a construction process used in building skyscraper cores; concrete is poured into movable wooden frames, and steel reinforcing bars are placed inside the frames for added strength

Slurry—a mixture of water and clay, or some other sediment

Snow load—the force caused by the snow

Soffit—the underside of an arch, eave, or other overhang

Solder—an alloy with a low melting point that is used to join metals

Soldering—a process whereby two pieces of metal are joined by the melting of a solder between them

Solid—a firm mass with a clear size, shape, and volume; not a gas or liquid

Sound wave—a pattern of air disturbance caused by energy as it passes through air (or some other medium) away from the source of the sound

Spread footing—a long and shallow supporting foundation element, for buildings or bridges; typically constructed using reinforced concrete

Stainless steel—high-grade steel with a lower than normal carbon content

Straw bale construction—a method of construction that involves using bales of straw that comes from leftover crops for both structure and infill

Substation—power equipment that lowers the voltage of incoming electricity to the levels at which it can be distributed to buildings and residences

Sway (noun)—side-to-side movement; specifically, in skyscrapers, caused by wind force

Task lighting—a lighting design for a building's interior that involves specific lights for specific tasks

Terra-cotta—clay that has been baked but not fully fired

Transformer—power equipment that changes the voltage of electricity by either raising or lowering it

Transmitter—an electronic device that sends a signal

Truss—a framework of beams that is shaped to form a rigid structure

Tuned mass damper—a heavy (400 tons plus) concrete block placed on one of the upper floors of a building to help resist sway from earthquakes and wind

Vacuum—a space that is completely empty and therefore has zero pressure

Viscous—describes a liquid whose thickness prevents easy flow

Welding—process in which two pieces of metal are permanently connected using heat

Wind load—the force caused by the wind

Work—transfer of energy from one object to another

FIND OUT MORE

Books

Ambrose, James. *Simplified Building Design for Wind and Earthquake Forces.* Hoboken, NJ: Wiley, 1997.

Bromann, Mark. *The Design and Layout of Fire Sprinkler Systems.* Boca Raton, FL: CRC, 2001.

Cowan, David. *Great Chicago Fires: Historic Blazes That Shaped a City.* Chicago: Lake Claremont Press, 2001.

Creative Publishing International. *Basic Wiring & Electrical Repair.* Chanhassen, MN: Creative Publishing International, 1991.

Kamin, Blair. *Why Architecture Matters: Lessons from Chicago.* Chicago: University of Chicago Press, 2003.

Khan, Yasmin. *Building Blocks: The John Hancock Center.* Princeton, NJ: Princeton Architectural Press, 2000.

Nash, Eric. *Manhattan Skyscrapers.* Princeton, NJ: Princeton Architectural Press, 1999.

Randall, Frank. *The History of Development of Building Construction in Chicago.* Champaign: University of Illinois Press, 1999.

Traister, John. *Commercial Electrical Wiring.* Carlsbad, CA: Craftsman Book Company, 2000.

Web sites

Cesar Pelli: www.cesar-pelli.com

Chemistry: www.chemistry.about.com

The Chief Engineer: www.chiefengineer.org

Eiffel Tower: www.tour-eiffel.fr

Empire State Building: www.esbnyc.com

Emporis Data Standards: corporate.emporis.com

Encyclopedia of Chicago: www.encyclopedia.chicagohistory.org

Eric Weisstein's World of Physics: www.scienceworld.wolfram.com/physics/

How Stuff Works: www.howstuffworks.com

Los Angeles Fire Department: www.lafire.com

Mechanical Engineering Design Guide: www.engineershandbook.com

Monadnock Building: www.monadnockbuilding.com

National Glass Association: www.glass.org/indres/info.htm

Otis Elevator Company: www.otis.com

Palmolive Building: www.palmolivebuilding.com

PBS American Experience, The Telephone: www.pbs.org/wgbh/amex/telephone

Petronas: www.petronas.com.my

Physics Classroom: www.glenbrook.k12.il.us/GBSSCI/PHYS/Class/BBoard.html

Sears Tower: www.thesearstower.com

Skidmore Owings and Merrill: www.som.com

Specialty Steel Industry of North America: www.ssina.com

Stainless Steel World: www.stainless-steel-world.net

The Stubbins Associates: www.stubbins.us

Telephony Museum: www.telephonymuseum.com

Trump World Tower: www.wikipedia.org/wiki/Trump

Wisconsin Engineer: www.engr.wisc.edu

Woolworth's Virtual Museum: museum.woolworths.co.uk

INDEX

Page numbers in italics refer to illustrations.